MAYER SMITH

The Silent Investor

Copyright © 2025 by Mayer Smith

All rights reserved. No part of this publication may be reproduced, stored or transmitted in any form or by any means, electronic, mechanical, photocopying, recording, scanning, or otherwise without written permission from the publisher. It is illegal to copy this book, post it to a website, or distribute it by any other means without permission.

This novel is entirely a work of fiction. The names, characters and incidents portrayed in it are the work of the author's imagination. Any resemblance to actual persons, living or dead, events or localities is entirely coincidental.

Mayer Smith asserts the moral right to be identified as the author of this work.

Mayer Smith has no responsibility for the persistence or accuracy of URLs for external or third-party Internet Websites referred to in this publication and does not guarantee that any content on such Websites is, or will remain, accurate or appropriate.

Designations used by companies to distinguish their products are often claimed as trademarks. All brand names and product names used in this book and on its cover are trade names, service marks, trademarks and registered trademarks of their respective owners. The publishers and the book are not associated with any product or vendor mentioned in this book. None of the companies referenced within the book have endorsed the book.

First edition

*This book was professionally typeset on Reedsy.
Find out more at reedsy.com*

Contents

1	The Hidden Offer	1
2	Barista for Hire	6
3	The First Shift	13
4	Secrets and Setbacks	21
5	Brewing Tensions	30
6	Cracks in the Armor	39
7	Shattered Trust	48
8	Under the Surface	55
9	Breaking Point	62
10	Fractured Foundations	69
11	Glimmer of Hope	76
12	The Choice	83
13	Last Stand	90
14	The Breaking Point	97
15	Consequence of Choice	104
16	Final Hour	111
17	Calm Before the Storm	118
18	Final Gamble	125
19	Breaking Forth	132
20	Final Decision	139

One

The Hidden Offer

The rain drummed steadily against the glass windows of Ethan Sinclair's high-rise office, the city lights reflecting off the polished wood of his desk. The skyline stretched endlessly beyond him, a glittering testament to the empire he had built. Billionaire. Investor. Powerhouse. These were the titles the world had given him, but tonight, he wasn't feeling the weight of his success.

He exhaled slowly, rolling the tumbler of whiskey between his fingers as he stared at the report on his desk. The bold red letters at the top of the page caught his eye again.

Sienna's Brew – Business at Risk of Closure

Ethan had read hundreds of reports like this before. Small businesses on the brink of collapse, crushed beneath the weight of market competition, poor management, or simply bad luck. Normally, he would skim through, assess potential investment opportunities, and move on. But something about this one had made him pause.

The café was nothing spectacular on paper. It was a small, independently owned coffee shop tucked between towering buildings in a gentrified part of town. A relic in an evolving neighborhood. The financials were grim—declining revenue, overdue payments, and a predatory lease agreement that threatened to force the owner out within months.

But it wasn't the numbers that caught his attention. It was the name behind the business.

Sienna Carter.

Ethan leaned back in his chair, his gaze drifting toward the floor-to-ceiling windows that overlooked the city. He had never met her, but he knew her type. Stubborn. Passionate. The kind of person who fought against corporate greed without ever realizing that, sometimes, power was necessary for survival.

He picked up the folder, flipping through the pages again, his eyes lingering on a black-and-white photograph paperclipped to the last page.

She wasn't smiling. Unlike the polished business portraits he was used to seeing, this one was different—probably taken from a local newspaper article. A woman in her late twenties, her dark curls wild from the wind, stood in front of the café with her arms crossed over her apron. Her expression was fierce, determined, a slight challenge hidden in her eyes. The article beneath it was titled: "Big Coffee vs. The Little Guy—One Woman's Fight to Keep Her Business Alive."

Ethan smirked. "So, you hate people like me," he murmured, setting the paper down.

A sharp knock at the door interrupted his thoughts. His assistant, Claire, stepped inside, her usual crisp efficiency evident in the way she carried herself.

"The Perrault Coffee deal has gone through," she announced, setting another folder on his desk. "They're opening three new locations downtown. Should give them a solid market share."

Ethan barely glanced at it. "They're opening one near Sienna's Brew, aren't they?"

Claire hesitated. "Yes. It'll be their biggest competitor."

He nodded, already knowing the answer. "And she won't survive it."

Silence stretched between them. Claire had worked with him long enough to sense when he was thinking something over.

"What are you going to do?" she asked carefully.

Ethan traced a finger over the photograph. "Buy the building."

Claire blinked. "You want to acquire the café?"

"No." His voice was smooth, deliberate. "I want to buy the building, pay off her debts, and keep her from knowing I'm behind it. If Perrault tries to push her out, I'll make sure she has the upper hand."

Claire hesitated for only a moment before nodding. "I'll make the arrangements."

She turned to leave, but Ethan spoke again.

"One more thing," he said, pushing the file toward her. "Find me a way in."

She frowned. "In?"

"I want to see the café. Work there, if possible. Undercover."

Claire stared at him, stunned for the first time in years. "You want to work as a barista?"

"I want to understand why she's fighting so hard." His lips curled slightly. "And if I'm going to help her, I need to know exactly what she's up against."

Claire let out a breath, clearly biting back her questions. "Alright," she said finally. "I'll make it happen."

When the door clicked shut behind her, Ethan leaned back in his chair, exhaling slowly.

The Hidden Offer

This wasn't just another investment.

This was something different.

And he wasn't sure if that excited him—or terrified him.

Two

Barista for Hire

E than Sinclair had walked into boardrooms worth billions, shaken hands with the world's most powerful executives, and made decisions that shifted entire industries. Yet, as he stood outside Sienna's Brew, staring at the rain-slicked sign above the door, he felt an unfamiliar sensation settle in his chest.

Doubt.

The café was smaller than he had imagined. Nestled between two larger buildings, it looked almost out of place—like something stubbornly holding on against the inevitable tide of progress. The large glass window showcased a warm interior, dimly lit with Edison bulbs strung across the ceiling. Wooden tables, slightly worn but charming, lined the walls, and the air smelled of fresh espresso and something sweet, possibly cinnamon.

A small "HELP WANTED" sign was taped to the glass near the entrance. Claire had told him about it. That was his way in.

Taking a breath, Ethan pushed open the door, and a soft chime rang above him. The smell of coffee deepened, mingling with something floral—probably from the tiny vase of wildflowers on the counter.

It was late afternoon, and only a handful of customers sat scattered around, tucked into corners with their laptops or books. A lone barista stood behind the counter, her back to him as she worked the espresso machine.

And then she turned.

Sienna Carter.

For a brief second, he was caught off guard. The woman in the newspaper photo hadn't done her justice. Up close, there was something striking about her—sharp, intelligent eyes the color of rich hazelnut, dark curls pulled into a messy bun, and an air of effortless confidence. But her exhaustion was just as evident. There were faint shadows under her eyes, a weary tension in her shoulders.

She glanced at him, barely registering his presence as she turned back to the machine. "Be right with you."

Ethan took the moment to compose himself, adjusting the strap of the old leather messenger bag Claire had forced on him to complete the "broke, job-seeking man" look.

Finally, Sienna turned again, this time actually looking at him. Her gaze flickered over him, assessing, and he could practically hear her thoughts.

Too clean. Too put together. Doesn't look like someone desperate for a barista job.

He needed to sell this.

"I saw the sign," he said, keeping his voice steady but casual. "You're hiring?"

Her expression remained neutral, but there was a flicker of skepticism. "Do you have experience?"

Lie convincingly. Keep it simple.

"Some."

Sienna folded her arms, looking unimpressed. "Where?"

Ethan hesitated, then rattled off the name of a café he had once acquired and flipped years ago. It wasn't a lie, not exactly.

She arched a brow. "Never heard of it."

He shrugged. "It was a small place."

She sighed, rubbing her temple. "Look, I'll be honest. I don't have time to train someone from scratch. My last barista quit unexpectedly, and I'm barely holding things together as it is."

"I learn fast," Ethan offered. "And I need the job."

That part wasn't a lie either. He did need the job—just not for the reasons she assumed.

Sienna studied him again, longer this time, as if trying to peel back whatever layers he was hiding. He held her gaze, steady but not too challenging. He had negotiated billion-dollar deals in the past, but this moment felt strangely more important.

She exhaled sharply. "Fine. Trial shift. Two hours. If you don't completely screw up, we'll talk."

He nodded. "Deal."

She motioned him behind the counter and tossed an apron his way. "Name?"

For the briefest second, he considered using his real name. But no.

"Ethan Shaw," he said smoothly, slipping the apron over his head.

"Alright, Ethan Shaw," she said, tightening her ponytail. "Let's see if you can make a cup of coffee without burning the place down."

The Silent Investor

—-

It turned out, making coffee was a lot harder than he thought.

Ethan had assumed there would be some kind of grace period—a bit of observation before jumping in. He was wrong.

"Double espresso, oat milk, extra shot," Sienna called out as she handed him his first order ticket. "You have exactly sixty seconds before the next order comes in."

He stared at the machine in front of him. Steam hissed, buttons blinked, and somewhere beneath it all, he knew it was supposed to be simple—grind, tamp, extract, steam milk. But nothing about this felt simple.

He hesitated for only a second before reaching for the portafilter. He overfilled it. Tamped it unevenly. When he locked it into place and started the extraction, the coffee dripped too slowly.

Sienna was watching.

"This is painful to watch," she muttered, stepping in beside him. "Here. Stop overfilling it. You're suffocating the espresso."

She reached past him, fingers brushing his briefly as she adjusted the dose and tamped with swift precision. He caught a hint of her scent—coffee, vanilla, something faintly citrus.

"Try again," she instructed.

He followed her lead, and this time, the espresso came out better. Still not perfect, but better.

She eyed it, then nodded. "Not completely hopeless."

Ethan smirked. "High praise."

She ignored that. "Now, milk. Do not scald it."

Spoiler: He scalded it.

Sienna groaned. "You just murdered the oat milk."

"Should I hold a funeral?"

Her lips twitched, as if she wanted to smile but refused to let herself. "Just try again."

By the time his trial shift neared its end, Ethan had fumbled his way through four orders, learned exactly how not to steam milk, and nearly knocked over a full tray of pastries.

He expected Sienna to tell him to leave. That he wasn't cut out for this.

Instead, she crossed her arms, assessing him. "You're a disaster."

Ethan wiped his hands on a towel. "Thanks."

"But," she continued, "you didn't quit. And you didn't try to argue when I corrected you."

"Would it have helped if I did?"

"No. I would have fired you on the spot."

Ethan chuckled. "Noted."

She sighed, clearly debating something, then finally extended her hand. "Shift tomorrow. 6 AM. If you're late, don't bother showing up."

He took her hand, shaking it firmly. "I'll be here."

As she pulled away, her gaze lingered on him just a second longer. Not suspicion exactly, but something close to it.

Ethan knew the hardest part wasn't learning how to be a barista.

The hardest part was making sure she never found out who he really was.

Three

The First Shift

The air outside was crisp, the kind of morning cold that seeped into bones and made city streets feel quieter than they should. Ethan Sinclair—now Ethan Shaw—stood outside Sienna's Brew, gripping a takeaway cup of coffee from a competitor's café down the street. Ironic. He had gotten up early, too early, unable to shake the restless energy vibrating through him.

A billionaire pretending to be a barista. The thought was still ridiculous, even to him.

He took a final sip of the too-sweet coffee before tossing it in the trash. The moment his hand touched the café's door handle, a strange sort of anticipation twisted in his chest.

He had made high-stakes deals, crushed negotiations, and

navigated the brutal world of finance. And yet, stepping into this felt like something entirely different.

The bell above the door jingled softly.

Inside, the café was dim, the morning light barely filtering through the windows. The scent of coffee, vanilla, and something faintly floral filled the space. Sienna was already behind the counter, pulling shots of espresso with sharp precision, her dark curls barely tamed into a ponytail. She didn't look up immediately, too focused on the task at hand.

"You're two minutes early," she said, her voice edged with the grogginess of someone who had been up for hours.

"Would you have fired me if I was two minutes late?" Ethan asked, slipping behind the counter.

Sienna glanced at him, her gaze appraising. "Absolutely."

A grin threatened to tug at his lips, but he smothered it. Instead, he reached for an apron, tying it securely around his waist. The fabric felt foreign, the role even more so.

"I'll be honest," Sienna said, adjusting the steam wand on the espresso machine. "I don't have time to babysit you today. Mornings are our busiest hours. You screw up an order, you remake it. No complaints, no shortcuts."

He nodded. "Got it."

The First Shift

She hesitated, as if she wanted to say something else, but then the first customer walked in, and just like that, the rush began.

—-

Ethan barely had time to think.

The orders came fast—lattes, cappuccinos, macchiatos, cold brews, mochas. There was no room for hesitation. Sienna barked out drink names, and he scrambled to keep up, his hands fumbling over the espresso machine.

The first latte he made was a disaster. He oversteamed the milk, resulting in a foamy mess that looked more like a science experiment than a drink.

"No. Again," Sienna ordered, dumping it down the sink without hesitation.

He gritted his teeth and tried again.

The next one wasn't much better, but it was passable. Barely.

By the time the line snaked toward the door, Ethan was sweating. He wasn't used to this—working with his hands, making something real instead of moving numbers on a screen. The pressure was different.

He burned his fingers twice. Scalded the milk once. Nearly dropped a ceramic cup.

At one point, Sienna sighed in frustration. "You have the coordination of a drunk raccoon."

Ethan huffed out a breath. "Great motivational coaching."

"You want motivation? Don't mess up the next order," she said flatly, nodding toward the waiting customer.

He turned back to the espresso machine, focusing. Stay calm. Stay sharp.

The next order—an Americano—was simple enough. Black coffee, hot water, no milk, no foam. Hard to mess up. He handed it over, and the customer gave him a nod of approval before heading toward the seating area.

Sienna arched a brow. "There's hope for you yet."

He smirked. "Don't sound so excited."

But before she could reply, the door swung open again, and a new customer stepped inside.

A man in an expensive suit. Sharp. Confident. The kind of person Ethan would have met in one of his real-life boardrooms. But that wasn't what caught his attention.

It was the logo on the man's travel mug.

Perrault Coffee.

The First Shift

Ethan stiffened.

Sienna's expression darkened the moment she saw it.

The man stepped up to the counter, his smile polished, practiced. "Sienna Carter," he said smoothly, as if greeting an old friend.

She folded her arms. "Julian."

Ethan kept his expression blank, but internally, the name rang a bell. Julian Marks. Executive at Perrault Coffee. One of the men pushing for aggressive expansion in the area. He had seen his name in reports before.

Julian glanced around the café, as if appraising it. "Busy morning, I see."

Sienna's jaw tightened. "What do you want?"

"I was in the neighborhood," Julian said casually. "Thought I'd stop by. Support small businesses."

Ethan had met enough corporate types to recognize the veiled insult. Small business. Temporary. Something that could be bought out or crushed.

Sienna saw it too.

"Not interested," she said, already turning away.

Julian sighed, as if dealing with a stubborn child. "Come on, Sienna. Just hear me out. Perrault is opening a new location down the block—"

"I know," she cut in.

"Then you also know that when we open, foot traffic here is going to drop significantly." He leaned against the counter. "I'm offering you a way out before that happens."

Ethan's hands curled into fists at his sides, but he forced himself to stay silent.

Sienna's face remained unreadable, but there was fire behind her eyes. "I don't need a way out."

Julian smiled. "Sienna. Be smart about this." He reached into his pocket and pulled out a neatly folded document, setting it on the counter. "A buyout. Generous terms. More than fair. You could walk away with enough to start fresh somewhere else."

Sienna didn't even look at it. Instead, she picked it up, crumpled it, and tossed it directly into the trash.

A muscle in Julian's jaw twitched. "That was unnecessary."

"No," Sienna said coolly. "What's unnecessary is you coming into my café, drinking my coffee, and trying to buy me out like I'm some desperate sellout."

Julian's smile faded. The mask slipped, just for a second. "Don't be naive, Sienna. The numbers don't lie. When we open, your profits will take a hit you can't recover from."

"I'll take my chances."

A tense silence stretched between them. Ethan could feel the weight of it, the unspoken challenge in the air.

Finally, Julian exhaled sharply and straightened his tie. "Your stubbornness is admirable. Stupid, but admirable." He turned toward the door but paused, glancing at Ethan for the first time. His gaze flickered over him—assessing, curious.

"You're new," Julian said.

Ethan met his gaze evenly. "That's right."

Julian's smile was sharp. "Good luck working here. You'll need it."

With that, he left, the door swinging shut behind him.

Sienna let out a long breath, rubbing her temples. Ethan studied her, the tension in her shoulders, the quiet frustration in her eyes.

"You okay?" he asked.

She looked at him, as if remembering he was still there. Her expression softened—just slightly.

"I will be," she muttered, grabbing a fresh order ticket. "Now stop standing around and make yourself useful."

Ethan smirked, picking up the next order.

It was only his first shift, and already, the battle lines had been drawn.

This was going to be interesting.

Four

Secrets and Setbacks

The morning rush at Sienna's Brew had finally eased, leaving behind the scent of espresso and caramelized sugar hanging thick in the air. Ethan stood behind the counter, rolling his sleeves up, his fingers still dusted with coffee grounds. His muscles ached from the constant movement—pulling shots, steaming milk, rushing orders—but exhaustion was the last thing on his mind.

Instead, his thoughts kept circling back to Julian Marks and the way Sienna had practically burned a hole through him with her glare.

She wasn't just resisting Perrault Coffee. She was at war with it.

And Ethan couldn't stop wondering why.

Sienna, on the other hand, had barely spoken since Julian left. She moved with calculated precision, wiping down counters, checking inventory, pretending the encounter hadn't rattled her. But Ethan had spent years reading people, picking apart their defenses.

She was shaken.

"Do they come by often?" he asked, breaking the silence.

Sienna paused for half a second before resuming her task. "Who?"

"You know who."

Her jaw tightened, but she didn't look at him. "Julian? No. Not personally. But Perrault Coffee? They're always lurking."

Ethan leaned against the counter, watching her. "Seems personal."

This time, she did glance at him, eyes sharp. "It is."

Something about the way she said it made Ethan want to press further, but before he could, the door swung open again, and an older woman in a thick scarf stepped inside.

"Morning, Sienna, darling," the woman called out, her voice warm and familiar.

Sienna immediately brightened, dropping the rag she was

holding. "Mrs. Carmichael!"

The woman—Mrs. Carmichael, apparently—shuffled over to the counter, smiling at Ethan before turning her attention back to Sienna. "How's business, dear?"

Sienna hesitated. The pause was almost imperceptible, but Ethan caught it.

"Busy," she answered finally. "As always."

Mrs. Carmichael patted her hand. "I do worry about you, you know. That nasty Perrault Coffee coming in, trying to stomp out all the little places like this."

Sienna forced a smile. "I'm not going anywhere."

The older woman hummed, unconvinced, then turned her gaze to Ethan. "And who's this? A new face?"

Ethan wiped his hands on a towel and extended one. "Ethan Shaw."

Mrs. Carmichael took his hand, giving him an approving nod. "Well, it's good to see a new set of hands around here. This place could use it."

Ethan arched a brow. "That bad?"

Mrs. Carmichael's smile faltered, just for a second.

The Silent Investor

Sienna cut in before she could answer. "Mrs. Carmichael, your usual?"

The woman sighed but let it go. "Yes, dear. And put an extra shot in. I need it today."

As Sienna busied herself with the order, Ethan watched the older woman carefully. She lingered near the counter, tapping her fingers against the wood, her eyes scanning the café like she was committing it to memory.

"Do you come here often?" Ethan asked, keeping his tone light.

Mrs. Carmichael chuckled. "More than I should. Sienna makes the best coffee in the city."

Sienna scoffed. "That's because you refuse to go anywhere else."

Mrs. Carmichael smiled but didn't argue. Instead, she lowered her voice. "There's not a lot of places like this left, you know. The big chains are swallowing them up one by one."

Ethan nodded, but he didn't respond.

Because he was one of those big chains.

And if Sienna ever found out, he doubted she'd just toss him out—she'd probably set him on fire first.

Her voice broke through his thoughts. "Ethan, can you grab the sugar syrup from the back?"

"On it."

He slipped through the swinging door into the back storage room, where shelves lined the walls, stocked with coffee beans, syrups, and cleaning supplies. A small desk sat in the corner, papers stacked haphazardly across it.

Ethan's eyes landed on them immediately.

He shouldn't. He shouldn't.

But he did.

Stepping closer, he scanned the topmost paper. Invoices. Orders for supplies. Rent statements. His gaze snagged on one line in particular.

Final Notice – Overdue Balance.

His stomach tightened.

Sienna was in deeper trouble than she let on.

Footsteps approached. Ethan barely managed to step back before the door swung open, and Sienna appeared, giving him a quizzical look.

"You find it?"

He grabbed the nearest bottle of syrup and held it up. "Right here."

She studied him for a second longer before nodding. "Good. Let's go."

He followed her out, but his mind was already turning.

Sienna didn't just have a rivalry with Perrault Coffee. She was drowning.

And he was the only reason she wasn't sinking completely.

But she didn't know that.

And she could never, ever find out.

—-

The afternoon dragged on, the café gradually quieting as the lunch crowd trickled out. Sienna had barely stopped moving all day, and Ethan was beginning to wonder if she had an off switch.

At one point, she was standing on a chair, replacing a lightbulb in the ceiling fixture when the door chime rang again.

A man stepped inside. Tall, broad-shouldered, dark hair. Late forties, early fifties.

Sienna's entire body stiffened.

Ethan felt it before he even turned to see her expression. A tightness in the air, like a wire pulled too tight.

The man's lips curled into a slow, calculated smile. "Sienna."

She climbed down from the chair, her movements careful, deliberate. "What are you doing here?"

The man shrugged, stepping further inside. "Can't a father visit his daughter?"

Ethan blinked. Father?

Sienna's fingers curled into fists at her sides. "You don't visit. You don't call. You don't exist."

The man chuckled, but there was no warmth in it. "Still dramatic, I see." His gaze flicked toward Ethan. "Who's this?"

Sienna's voice was sharp. "My employee. None of your business."

Ethan folded his arms, stepping slightly closer. He wasn't sure why he did it—whether it was to shield her from whatever history lingered between them or just to make sure she wasn't handling it alone.

The man ignored him, turning his attention back to Sienna. "You got my letter?"

"I got it," she said flatly.

"And?"

Sienna crossed her arms. "And the answer's the same as before. No."

A muscle in the man's jaw twitched. "You're being stubborn."

"No," Sienna said quietly. "I'm being smart."

The silence between them was thick, charged.

Finally, the man exhaled, stepping back. "Fine. Have it your way. But don't come running when this place collapses."

And just like that, he turned and walked out, the door swinging shut behind him.

Ethan turned to Sienna, but her expression was locked down, unreadable.

"You okay?" he asked.

She let out a slow breath, running a hand through her hair. "I'm fine."

Liar.

But Ethan didn't push. Not yet.

Instead, he nodded toward the door. "Who was that?"

Sienna met his gaze, and for the first time, he saw something unguarded there.

Secrets and Setbacks

A quiet kind of pain.

"My father," she said. Then, more quietly, "Or at least, he used to be."

And with that, she walked away.

Ethan watched her go, his mind spinning.

Sienna was fighting more battles than he realized.

And for some reason, he was starting to care a little too much.

Five

Brewing Tensions

The air inside Sienna's Brew was heavy, thick with the scent of espresso and something far less tangible—unspoken tension.

Ethan had spent enough time in high-stakes negotiations to recognize when someone was on edge, and Sienna Carter was practically radiating it. She hadn't spoken a word about her father since he left the café yesterday. She hadn't acknowledged his visit, hadn't made any offhand comments or sarcastic jabs.

Nothing.

And that silence said more than words ever could.

It gnawed at Ethan as he worked the espresso machine, the rhythmic grind of coffee beans a temporary distraction. The

Brewing Tensions

café wasn't busy yet. The morning rush hadn't begun, leaving them in the strange quiet before the chaos.

Sienna stood near the front window, wiping the already-clean glass with unnecessary force.

"You're going to shatter it if you keep that up," Ethan remarked, keeping his tone light.

Sienna stiffened slightly before lowering the cloth. "Just making sure there's no streaks."

Ethan shot her a look. "Right. That must be it."

She turned, arching a brow. "You got something to say, Shaw?"

He did. Plenty. But he wasn't about to push her into a conversation she wasn't ready to have.

Instead, he shrugged. "Just making an observation."

Sienna studied him for a moment, her expression unreadable. Then, without another word, she tossed the cloth onto the counter and disappeared into the back room.

Yeah. Definitely not fine.

Ethan exhaled slowly, watching the door swing shut behind her. Every instinct he had told him to let it go. He barely knew her. This wasn't his business.

But he wanted to make it his business.

And that was the real problem.

—-

The morning rush arrived like a tidal wave.

One minute, the café was quiet. The next, it was chaos.

Customers flooded in, orders piled up, and the sound of steaming milk and clinking mugs filled the air. Ethan barely had time to think.

Sienna was back to her usual self—sharp, focused, efficient. She called out orders, handled customers with effortless charm, and moved behind the counter with the kind of ease that only came from years of practice.

But there was something off.

She wasn't talking to him. Not like she usually did.

No sarcastic quips. No annoyed sighs. No subtle digs at his less-than-stellar barista skills.

And that? That was weird.

Ethan wasn't sure why it bothered him so much, but it did.

At one point, he nearly overfilled a cappuccino, his attention slipping for half a second. Sienna caught it instantly.

"Careful," she said, her voice tight. "You're flooding the foam."

Ethan adjusted, correcting his mistake, but instead of firing back with his usual dry remark, he just nodded.

"Got it."

Sienna blinked, as if surprised by his lack of response. But before she could say anything else, the bell above the door rang, and a new customer stepped in.

Ethan didn't recognize her.

But Sienna did.

He saw it immediately—the way her entire body stilled, the way her fingers curled slightly against the countertop.

The woman was tall, blonde, and expensive. Everything about her screamed high-end—her tailored blazer, her designer handbag, the way she carried herself like she owned the entire block.

She didn't even glance at the menu.

Instead, she walked right up to the counter, smiling.

"Sienna," she said, voice smooth, practiced. "It's been a while."

Sienna's expression didn't change. "Not long enough."

Ethan's curiosity flared instantly. Who the hell was this?

The blonde woman smirked. "Still holding a grudge, I see."

Sienna crossed her arms. "What do you want, Vanessa?"

Vanessa. Ethan committed the name to memory.

Vanessa let out a dramatic sigh, as if this whole encounter was exhausting for her. "I heard about Perrault moving in. Wanted to see how you were holding up."

Sienna's jaw clenched. "I'm fine."

Vanessa's gaze flickered around the café. "Really? Because from what I hear, this place is struggling."

Ethan tensed. Who the hell was this woman?

Sienna's expression remained icy. "I'm not interested in whatever you're selling."

Vanessa's smile widened. "Who said I was selling anything?" She leaned in slightly, lowering her voice. "You know, Perrault made me a very generous offer for my old café. You could do the same. Take the money, start fresh somewhere new."

Ethan's blood ran cold.

Brewing Tensions

Her old café?

Realization hit him like a freight train.

Vanessa used to own a coffee shop. And now, she worked for Perrault.

She had sold out.

And now she was trying to get Sienna to do the same.

Sienna let out a slow breath. "Not interested."

Vanessa tsked. "You're making this harder than it needs to be."

Ethan had heard enough.

Before he could stop himself, he stepped forward, placing a deliberate hand on the counter.

"She said she's not interested," he said smoothly.

Vanessa turned her attention to him for the first time, her eyes raking over him with mild curiosity. "And who are you?"

"Ethan," he replied evenly. "Barista."

Something flickered in her expression. "A barista." She turned back to Sienna, amused. "You've got employees fighting your battles for you now?"

Sienna's eyes darkened. "Ethan, don't."

But Ethan was already committed.

"Just seems like a waste of time," he said casually, tilting his head. "Trying to convince someone to sell when they've already told you to get lost."

Vanessa arched a perfectly manicured brow. "And you think you know how business works?"

Ethan smirked. "I think I know when someone's desperate."

Sienna stiffened beside him.

Vanessa's smile faltered just slightly. "Desperate?"

"Yeah." Ethan leaned in a little, lowering his voice just enough. "You already took the money once. You already sold out. So why are you here? Trying to convince someone else to make the same mistake?"

For a split second, something flashed in Vanessa's eyes—annoyance, maybe even anger.

Then, just as quickly, she smoothed it over, giving him a slow, calculating smile.

"Interesting," she murmured. "You've got some bite."

Ethan didn't blink. "Only when I need to."

Brewing Tensions

Vanessa exhaled sharply, then turned back to Sienna. "Fine. Have it your way."

She pulled a business card from her pocket, sliding it across the counter.

"If you ever change your mind, you know where to find me."

Sienna didn't touch the card. Didn't even look at it.

Vanessa smirked. "See you around, Sienna."

And just like that, she was gone.

The door swung shut behind her, and a heavy silence settled in the café.

Ethan exhaled, rubbing the back of his neck. "What the hell was that?"

Sienna's shoulders were tense. "That was Vanessa Pierce. Former café owner. Current Perrault puppet."

Ethan studied her. "She used to be your competition?"

Sienna let out a short, bitter laugh. "She used to be my friend."

The weight of those words hit him harder than he expected.

Sienna grabbed the business card from the counter, staring at it for a long moment. Then, without hesitation, she ripped it in half and tossed it into the trash.

Ethan watched her, something tightening in his chest.

She was fighting this war alone.

But maybe... she didn't have to.

Six

Cracks in the Armor

The tension from Vanessa's visit lingered in the air long after she left, clinging to the café like the last wisps of steam rising from an abandoned cup of coffee.

Sienna had thrown herself back into work with a single-minded intensity that would have been admirable—if it wasn't so obvious that she was trying to distract herself.

Ethan noticed every detail. The way she wiped the counters harder than necessary. The way she reorganized the pastry case twice, even though no customers had touched it. The way her shoulders tensed each time the doorbell chimed, as if she were bracing for another unwelcome visitor.

She was unraveling.

And Ethan couldn't stop himself from watching it happen.

For the first time since stepping into this café, since assuming his new identity as a clueless barista, he realized something: This wasn't just business for Sienna.

It was personal. Deeply personal.

And the more he saw, the more he realized he needed to know why.

—-

The late afternoon lull arrived like an exhausted sigh, leaving only a few customers scattered throughout the café. The sun was beginning to dip lower in the sky, casting long golden shadows across the wooden floors.

Ethan finished wiping down the espresso machine and turned to find Sienna hunched over a stack of paperwork near the register.

Invoices. Statements. Things she had no doubt been avoiding all day.

He didn't say anything at first, just observed. The crease in her brow. The way she tapped her pen against the counter, chewing on the end without realizing it.

And then, as if sensing his stare, she let out an annoyed sigh.

"What?"

Ethan shrugged. "Nothing. Just wondering if that pen tastes any good."

Sienna blinked, then glanced down at the pen between her fingers before scowling and tossing it onto the counter.

"Shut up."

Ethan smirked but didn't push further. Instead, he leaned against the counter, arms crossed. "You want to talk about it?"

She stiffened. "Talk about what?"

"The fact that you've been acting like a live wire since your dad showed up."

Her eyes darkened, but she kept her gaze fixed on the papers in front of her. "I'm fine."

"Right," Ethan drawled. "And I'm a world-class barista."

She shot him a glare, but there was no real heat behind it.

"I don't need to talk about it," she said, voice clipped.

Ethan watched her for a moment, then nodded. "Alright."

Sienna hesitated, as if expecting him to push her further. When he didn't, she exhaled slowly and refocused on the paperwork.

Ethan waited a beat before speaking again. "So… you and Vanessa?"

Sienna's grip tightened around the papers. "What about us?"

"You said you used to be friends."

Her jaw clenched. "We were."

"What happened?"

Sienna didn't answer right away. She just stared at the papers in front of her, like she was seeing something else entirely.

Then, finally, she spoke.

"We started out at the same time," she murmured. "Both of us. Small café owners, trying to make it work in a city where places like Perrault dominate everything."

Ethan remained silent, letting her talk.

"For a while, it felt like we were on the same side. We'd share supplier tips, talk about struggling through slow seasons, warn each other when landlords tried to pull anything shady." She let out a humorless laugh. "We used to joke that we'd be the last two independent cafés standing, no matter what."

Ethan frowned. "So what changed?"

Sienna's fingers curled slightly against the countertop. "Perrault made her an offer. A big one."

"And she took it."

She nodded stiffly. "She didn't even hesitate. One day, she was fighting beside me. The next, she was gone."

Ethan exhaled slowly. "That must've hurt."

Sienna scoffed, shaking her head. "You know what the worst part is?"

He waited.

"She told me I was being stupid," she muttered. "That I was clinging to something that wasn't going to last. That fighting was pointless."

Ethan studied her carefully. "And you still believe it's not?"

She met his gaze, something fierce burning behind her eyes. "I know it's not."

And damn—there was something about the way she said it, something raw and unshakable, that made Ethan believe it too.

But before he could respond, the door chime rang again.

This time, the visitor was unexpected.

Ethan didn't recognize the man who stepped inside, but Sienna did.

Her entire posture changed in an instant. The fire in her eyes was replaced by something harder. Colder.

The man was tall, broad-shouldered, and had the look of someone who belonged in a boardroom, not a coffee shop. His suit was crisp, his expression unreadable. But his eyes—sharp and assessing—landed on Sienna like a target.

"Miss Carter," he said, voice smooth. "I was hoping to have a word."

Sienna set her pen down carefully. "If you're here about a buyout, save your breath."

The man didn't flinch. "I think you'll want to hear this."

Ethan tensed beside her. Who the hell was this guy?

Sienna folded her arms. "You have thirty seconds."

The man exhaled, as if dealing with an impatient child. "Perrault Coffee has finalized their lease."

Sienna didn't move. "I know."

"The construction starts next week," he continued. "You'll start losing foot traffic immediately."

Ethan clenched his jaw. Bastard.

Sienna's face remained unreadable. "Is that all?"

The man smiled, slow and deliberate. "No. I have an offer."

She rolled her eyes. "I already told Vanessa—"

"It's not the same offer," the man interrupted smoothly. "This one is better."

Silence stretched between them.

Ethan hated the way the man said it.

Like he already knew what her answer would be. Like he knew she was desperate.

Sienna tilted her head slightly. "Better, how?"

The man slid a folder onto the counter.

Inside, Ethan could see the crisp edges of a contract.

"You're a fighter, Miss Carter," the man said. "I respect that."

Sienna didn't touch the folder.

"But business isn't about fighting," he continued. "It's about knowing when to stop."

The Silent Investor

Ethan's hands curled into fists.

Sienna was silent for a long time.

Then, slowly, deliberately, she picked up the folder.

And tore it straight down the middle.

The man's expression flickered—just for a fraction of a second—before smoothing over again.

Sienna leaned forward, resting her palms on the counter. "You can tell Perrault that they can build their soulless little coffee factory wherever they want. But this?" She gestured around the café. "This is mine."

Ethan had never respected anyone more.

The man exhaled through his nose, clearly unimpressed. "Suit yourself," he said, brushing imaginary dust from his sleeve.

Then, with a final glance toward Ethan—an odd, lingering look—he turned and walked out.

The café door swung shut behind him, the bell jingling like the end of a war drum.

Ethan let out a breath he hadn't realized he was holding.

Sienna straightened, rolling her shoulders back. "Well."

Ethan arched a brow. "That was fun."

She snorted.

But as she turned away, Ethan caught something in her expression.

She was still standing.

Still fighting.

But for how much longer?

And for the first time, Ethan wondered…

What would happen if she lost?

Seven

Shattered Trust

Ethan sat at the counter, his fingers tapping an unconscious rhythm against the wooden surface. The café was quieter now, the last of the customers having left, but his mind was anything but still. He had watched Sienna stand her ground against the man from Perrault Coffee with a kind of determination that was both awe-inspiring and... unsettling.

There was something about the way she faced down people—how she put up these walls, so perfectly crafted, so impenetrable, that Ethan found it almost impossible to know what was real beneath them.

She had been fighting this war for so long, and yet, each time someone threw something her way, she absorbed the blows with an ironclad resolve. But Ethan could see the cracks in her armor. He had seen them all day: the way her hands shook when she thought no one was watching, the way her jaw tightened when the door opened and she braced for another battle.

She wasn't invincible. Not by a long shot.

"Hey, you need anything?" Sienna's voice broke through his thoughts, and he looked up to see her standing a few feet away, holding a rag loosely in her hand, her expression unreadable.

Ethan smiled but it felt strained, almost forced. "I'm good. Just waiting for the place to quiet down."

Sienna nodded, her eyes flicking back to the empty tables. "Yeah. I'm not used to it being this quiet." There was a note of something raw in her voice—was it fear? Or something else? She wasn't making eye contact, though. Instead, her gaze was distant, staring at nothing in particular. She seemed... lost.

He didn't push her, just watched as she moved to clean up the counter again. She was trying to keep busy, trying to keep her mind from drifting to whatever nightmare had brought her to this point.

Ethan set his cup down with a soft clink, then stood, walking toward her slowly. He wasn't sure why he was doing this, but the impulse was there, a sharp pull in his chest. He couldn't just stand by and pretend everything was fine.

"Talk to me, Sienna," he said quietly.

She froze, the rag still in her hand. Her posture went rigid, and for a moment, he thought she might walk away from him again, the walls around her rising higher, thicker, stronger. But she didn't.

"I told you I'm fine," she muttered, her voice flat, devoid of the fire she usually carried.

"You're not fine," Ethan replied, the words slipping out before he could stop them. "You're not fine, and you know it."

Sienna took a deep breath, and when she spoke again, it wasn't to argue. It was a confession, soft and dangerous. "I can't keep doing this. I can't keep pretending like everything's okay. Like I'm still in control." Her hands clenched around the rag, twisting it into tight, painful folds. "I'm losing, Ethan. Every day, I'm losing."

The words hit him harder than he expected. He'd known it—he'd seen the way she fought, how much she was struggling—but to hear her admit it, to hear her voice crack with that raw emotion, sent a sharp pain through his chest.

"What do you mean by that?" he asked, stepping a little closer, careful not to crowd her.

Sienna met his gaze finally, and for a moment, it felt like she was seeing him for the first time—really seeing him. Her eyes were wide, vulnerable, full of something she hadn't let anyone see before. But the moment was fleeting, gone in the blink of an eye as she looked away again, her gaze dropping to the floor.

"I'm not going to win, Ethan," she said, her voice barely above a whisper. "Perrault's got the money, the power. They've got people who can make problems disappear. They have the resources to crush me, and I'm... I'm alone. I don't have anyone. No one to help me. No one who understands what it's like to run a place like this... to fight every day just to keep it alive." She shook her head, her frustration mounting. "And now I'm just dragging it all down with me."

Ethan's breath caught in his throat. Alone. It was a word he understood all too well. But what she didn't see, what she couldn't see, was that she wasn't alone. Not with him here. Not with the way he was starting to care far more than he had any right to.

He reached out, placing a hand gently on her shoulder, and she stiffened, but didn't pull away.

"You're not alone, Sienna," he said quietly. "I'm here."

She didn't respond immediately. Instead, she pulled away from his touch, the distance between them widening. But even as she stepped back, she seemed to shrink, as if she were trying to retreat into herself.

"I don't know if that helps," she said, her voice thick with bitterness. "You don't understand what it's like. You don't get what's at stake. You've never had to fight for something you love and watch it slip away, bit by bit. Perrault's playing chess, and I'm stuck here, moving pawns."

Ethan felt the sharp sting of her words, but he refused to back down. "Maybe I don't understand completely," he admitted, his voice low. "But I'm starting to. I'm starting to see what this place means to you. I see it every day when you open those doors and when you fight back against everything that's trying to crush you. And that's something worth fighting for. It's something worth saving."

Sienna shook her head, a frustrated laugh escaping her lips. "You don't know what it's like. You're just a guy working a shift behind the counter. You don't understand the pressure, the constant fear of failing. You don't know what it's like to have your whole life tied to something, only to watch it die in front of your eyes."

Her voice broke at the end of the sentence, and Ethan saw the cracks in her armor widen. She wasn't invincible, he had always known that. But seeing it in front of him—seeing her so vulnerable, so raw—made the pain in his chest unbearable.

He stepped closer again, his hand resting on the counter between them. "Sienna, I do get it. I'm not going to pretend like I know exactly what you're going through. But I do know what it's like to feel like everything is slipping away. To feel like you've lost control. I've been there, too."

She looked up at him sharply, and for a moment, they just stared at each other—two people caught in a moment of shared understanding.

And then, without warning, the door opened with a sharp jingle, breaking the fragile connection between them.

A man stepped inside. He was older, wearing a heavy coat that looked out of place in the warm café. His eyes were cold, calculating, and when he looked at Sienna, she stiffened immediately.

"Ms. Carter," the man said smoothly, his voice like polished steel. "I'm here to discuss business."

Ethan tensed, his hand instinctively reaching for something—anything—but the man's gaze flicked over him dismissively, ignoring him completely as he focused on Sienna.

"I already told you," Sienna said, her voice steady despite the way her entire body tensed. "I'm not interested."

The man didn't flinch. Instead, he reached into his coat pocket and pulled out a folded piece of paper. He slapped it on the counter between them, his eyes cold and unyielding.

"This is the final offer, Ms. Carter," he said. "I suggest you take it before things get... messy."

Ethan watched the folder on the counter, the tension thickening in the air. This was it. The breaking point.

Sienna didn't move, her face a mask of resolve, but the uncertainty in her eyes was impossible to miss.

Ethan stepped forward, his heart pounding, and placed a hand on the folder, sliding it away from Sienna's reach.

"I said no," Sienna replied, her voice cold and final.

But Ethan knew, deep down, that this wasn't over. And something told him that they were about to find out just how far Perrault was willing to go to get what they wanted.

And if Sienna was ready to lose everything.

Eight

Under the Surface

The night had fallen heavy and dark over the city. The streets outside Sienna's Brew glistened with the remnants of rain, reflecting the harsh glare of neon signs and headlights, but inside, the café was still—eerily quiet. The last customers had left an hour ago, leaving only the sounds of the hum of the refrigerators and the soft clink of Sienna's fingers tapping against the counter. She was standing behind the register, staring at the collection of papers that had been piling up over the past weeks—bills, invoices, reminders from suppliers. The lifeblood of the café was suffocating beneath the weight of financial strain.

Ethan was cleaning up behind the counter, wiping down surfaces he'd already wiped down a dozen times. His movements were automatic, almost robotic, as if his body had memorized the rhythm of the café. But his mind? It was miles away.

Every glance at Sienna told him how close she was to breaking, how her resolve was slowly cracking under the pressure. She was barely holding on, and yet she wouldn't let anyone—not even him—see the full extent of it.

Sienna hadn't spoken much since the man from Perrault Coffee had left earlier that evening, and Ethan could feel the air between them thick with unsaid words. He had never been good at reading people, but with Sienna, it wasn't hard. It wasn't the things she said that mattered—it was the things she didn't say.

He watched her now, the way her shoulders were tight, her brow furrowed as she shuffled through the paperwork. She was holding something back. And whatever it was, it was gnawing at her, like a constant pressure from within.

"Can I get you anything?" Ethan asked, his voice low, trying to break the silence. He knew it wasn't much, but it felt like the right thing to say.

Sienna didn't look up, her fingers still moving over the documents. "I'm fine," she replied, her tone flat.

Ethan didn't believe her. He wasn't sure he ever had.

He set the rag down and took a step toward her. "Sienna—"

"I said I'm fine," she interrupted, her voice sharp now, her eyes flickering up to meet his for a brief moment. The intensity in her gaze made his stomach tighten, a silent challenge in those dark eyes.

But Ethan wasn't backing down this time. He was tired of the walls. He was tired of the distance.

"No, you're not." His voice was quieter now, but there was an edge to it. "Look at you. You're not fine. You're falling apart, and you're pretending like everything's okay."

Sienna stiffened, the words hitting her like a slap. She quickly glanced away, trying to hide the vulnerability that had flashed in her eyes for a split second. The armor was back in place, but Ethan had already seen the cracks.

"Stop it," she muttered, rubbing her hands over her face as if to push away the emotions threatening to spill. "I don't have the energy for this, Ethan."

"You don't have the energy for what? For someone to care?" He stepped closer, frustration lacing his words. "You've been fighting this alone for too long. But you're not alone, Sienna. Not with me here."

She turned sharply to face him, her voice rising, the mask of control slipping for a moment. "You think I don't know that? You think I don't know how this looks? You think I haven't been fighting every day for years just to keep this place afloat? Just to keep myself afloat? And now… now it's slipping through my fingers." She took a step back, her hands trembling slightly as she clenched them into fists. "I don't have anything left. I don't know what else to do."

Ethan's heart twisted. He had seen the fight in her, the fierce independence, but hearing her speak like this… it shattered something inside him. It was the truth, the one she'd been hiding behind the walls for so long. And now, it was all spilling out in front of him.

"I'm not going to let you lose," he said quietly, stepping closer, his voice low but resolute. "Not like this."

She laughed bitterly, shaking her head. "You don't get it, Ethan. You're just here for a couple of shifts. You don't know the real cost of this. Of what I've sacrificed. The time. The energy. The money. I've been hanging by a thread for too long." Her voice cracked slightly, and she swallowed hard, trying to maintain some semblance of control. "And now Perrault is coming for me. They've got the money, the power. They'll crush me if I don't take their offer. And I—" She stopped herself abruptly, her breath catching.

Ethan's pulse quickened. "And what?"

She looked at him then, eyes wide, the walls she'd built around herself crumbling for just a moment. "And I'm not sure I can keep fighting anymore." Her voice was barely above a whisper. "I'm not sure I can keep it all together."

There it was. The vulnerability. The raw honesty that Sienna had been burying beneath her tough exterior for so long. Ethan stepped forward, his heart pounding.

"Sienna…" he started, but she held up a hand, cutting him off.

"Please. I don't want to talk about it." Her eyes closed, her face pale, her expression distant. "I just need some time. To think. To figure out what to do next."

Ethan stood there, the silence between them stretching, thick and suffocating. He knew she needed space. She was closing herself off again, retreating into that place where no one could reach her. But this time, Ethan wasn't going to let her.

He took a step closer, placing a hand on her arm gently. "You're not alone in this, Sienna. I don't care how much you want to push me away. I'm not going anywhere."

Sienna flinched at his touch, her body stiffening under his hand. Her eyes darted to his, and for the first time, he saw something— something that sent a chill down his spine. It was a fleeting look, but it was enough. It was fear. Fear of being hurt. Fear of letting someone in.

"I'm sorry," she said softly, her voice barely audible. "I don't know how to do this anymore."

Before he could respond, the door to the café opened, the familiar jingle of the bell cutting through the moment. Ethan turned instinctively, his hand still resting on Sienna's arm, but as the figure entered, a cold wave of recognition hit him.

It was Julian Marks.

The Perrault Coffee executive.

He stepped into the café like he owned the place, his eyes scanning the room before landing on Sienna. A cool, calculating smile spread across his face.

"Sienna," Julian said, his voice smooth as silk. "I thought I might find you here."

Ethan felt a surge of protective anger shoot through him, but he didn't move. He couldn't. Not yet. Sienna needed to handle this.

"Not interested," Sienna said without missing a beat, her voice hardening. "You've made your offer. Now leave."

Julian didn't budge, his smile only widening. "I think you'll find that the offer's getting better by the minute." He stepped closer, a folder in his hand, his eyes flicking to Ethan for a split second, dismissive. "Your café is worth more than you realize, Sienna. But time's running out. You need to decide. Soon."

Ethan's heart skipped a beat. There it was. The ultimatum. And Sienna's options were growing slimmer by the hour.

"I told you, I'm not selling," Sienna said, her voice unwavering now. She was trying to find that fire again, trying to push the fear down. But Ethan could see it—the cracks.

Julian, however, wasn't deterred. "You will," he said, his tone suddenly colder. "Because I'll make sure you do."

Ethan's hands balled into fists at his sides. But he didn't say anything. He couldn't. Not while Sienna was still in the fight.

The tension in the room was palpable, thick with unspoken threats. But then, without warning, Julian turned to leave, his footsteps echoing on the hardwood floor.

"I'll be back," he said over his shoulder, his voice dripping with menace. "You'll see."

As the door clicked shut behind him, Sienna let out a long breath, her body slumping as if the weight of the moment had finally hit her.

Ethan stayed where he was, watching her.

It was only a matter of time now. The walls were closing in on her. The question wasn't if she would fight—it was whether she could.

Nine

Breaking Point

The silence in Sienna's Brew was suffocating. Even the hum of the refrigerators, the soft buzz of the espresso machine left off after hours, and the distant sound of traffic outside couldn't fill the heavy, thick air between them.

Ethan stood at the counter, leaning forward slightly, watching Sienna with the same intensity that had marked every moment they'd shared since he'd stepped into this café as a complete stranger. There had been something undeniably magnetic about her from the start, something in the way she fought for this place, her passion fueling every action, every word. But now? The woman in front of him was different.

The fire was still there, but it was buried beneath layers of exhaustion and a growing despair that Ethan hadn't seen before. The walls were breaking.

Breaking Point

Sienna hadn't moved since Julian left hours ago. She hadn't spoken a word either. She simply stood in place, staring out the window, watching the city pass her by like a blurry memory. Her hands were clasped tightly in front of her, and her face was drawn tight with a quiet tension. She looked… fragile, in a way she never had before.

Ethan had watched people crumble under pressure, seen them fold in the face of corporate giants and ruthless competitors, but with Sienna, there was something about it that felt different. She wasn't just fighting for her business. She was fighting for herself.

And that, Ethan realized, was what scared her more than anything.

He didn't know how long they'd been standing there—minutes? Hours?—but the silence was unbearable. Finally, Ethan moved. He stepped toward the counter, his shoes clicking softly against the floor, and placed his hands down beside the papers she'd been staring at.

"You're going to drive yourself crazy if you keep doing that," he said, his voice low but firm.

Sienna didn't flinch, didn't look at him. She simply sighed, a soft, defeated sound that cut through him like a knife. "What's the point, Ethan? What's the point of all this? Of fighting?"

He blinked, his heart stuttering for a moment at the weariness in her tone. This was it. The moment when the relentless drive to survive collided with the cold reality of how deep she was in.

"Because you're not done yet," he said, his words steady, pushing through the quiet. "You've still got this place. You've still got the fight in you."

She finally turned her head, meeting his eyes, but there was nothing in her expression that was reassuring or hopeful. "You don't get it. Perrault is too big. I can't fight them forever. I can't even keep the doors open at this point. I don't know how much longer I can pretend like I've got it all under control." She shook her head, a sad smile crossing her lips, one that didn't reach her eyes. "I've been holding on for so long, Ethan. I'm running on fumes. And for what? To watch it all burn down in the end?"

Ethan's breath caught in his throat. That was it. The thing she'd been holding back all this time—the fear of losing everything, not just the café, but everything she'd put into it, every piece of herself. She'd built this place from nothing, and now she was watching it slip through her fingers. The weight of it was suffocating her.

He reached out instinctively, placing a hand gently on her shoulder. "You don't have to do this alone, Sienna."

She flinched, stepping back, and for a split second, Ethan thought she might walk away from him, that she might retreat into her self-imposed isolation again. But instead, her eyes softened, her shoulders sagging as the fight in her seemed to drain away.

"I don't know if I can keep doing it alone," she whispered, and for the first time, she looked vulnerable, like a person who had been battered and bruised by the weight of the world and had no idea how to rise above it anymore.

Ethan's heart clenched. "You don't have to. I'm right here."

Sienna shook her head, her lips trembling slightly. "I appreciate it, Ethan. I really do. But you don't know what this place means to me. You don't know how hard I've worked. How many nights I've stayed up wondering if I was crazy for thinking this could ever work. And now? It feels like it's all falling apart, piece by piece."

Ethan stepped closer, his voice softening. "Maybe I don't know everything, but I know one thing—this place matters. You matter. And I'm not going anywhere. I won't let Perrault take this from you."

Sienna's eyes flickered with something—maybe hope, maybe doubt, maybe both. She opened her mouth to say something, but the words caught in her throat just as the café door swung open, the bell ringing with a harsh jingle.

Ethan froze. The man who stepped inside was dressed sharply, too sharply. His presence felt like a shadow in the room, dark and unnerving. He was older, tall, with a confident but almost predatory air about him. The kind of man who didn't have to say much to make people uncomfortable.

The Silent Investor

It was him.

Graham Hunter.

Sienna had mentioned him before. The senior partner at Perrault Coffee, the one with the ruthless reputation for getting what he wanted, no matter the cost. He'd been pulling the strings in the background, making offers to Sienna for months now, trying to get her to sell out.

But this time… this time, Ethan could feel the weight of something darker behind his words.

Graham's eyes immediately found Sienna, and he smiled—a cold, calculated smile. "Sienna," he said, his voice smooth, almost too smooth. "I hope I'm not interrupting anything."

Sienna's body tensed, but she quickly recovered, putting the mask back on. "What do you want, Graham?"

His smile widened, and Ethan could practically feel the manipulative charm oozing off of him. "You've had my offer for weeks now," he said, glancing at the papers on the counter with a dismissive flick. "But I thought we should talk in person. You know, make sure you fully understand what's at stake."

"I understand perfectly," Sienna replied, her voice sharp but calm, betraying none of the emotions that Ethan knew were swirling underneath. "I told you before. I'm not interested."

Graham's gaze flicked briefly to Ethan before returning to

Sienna, the smile fading slightly. "You know, Sienna," he said, his voice lowering, "there's a point where stubbornness becomes a liability. You can keep fighting this, but it won't change anything. Perrault's already planned the expansion. The other locations are opening soon. This place"—he gestured around the café—"won't last. You'll be out of business in months."

Ethan felt a surge of anger, his pulse quickening. He was about to say something, to step in, but Sienna spoke first, her voice icy.

"This place isn't yours, Graham. And I'm not selling."

Graham's smile disappeared, replaced by something colder. His eyes narrowed as if he was seeing through her for the first time. "Fine," he said. "But don't say I didn't warn you." He turned on his heel and walked toward the door, his voice trailing behind him. "You'll be hearing from my lawyers."

As the door slammed shut behind him, the air in the café seemed to shift. The tension that had been so tightly wound between them snapped, and Ethan could see it in the way Sienna's shoulders slumped. Her entire posture sagged, like a balloon losing air, and for a brief moment, he could see just how close to the edge she was.

Ethan stepped forward, placing his hand gently on her arm. "Sienna... we need to talk."

But she shook her head, her voice barely a whisper. "There's nothing more to say. It's over."

Ethan stared at her, the weight of her words sinking in. She was giving up. She was really giving up.

But he wasn't going to let her.

"Not yet," he said, his voice firm but quiet. "It's not over. Not while I'm here."

Sienna didn't meet his eyes. Instead, she turned toward the window, the city lights reflecting in her glassy eyes. The fight was still in her—he could feel it. But it was buried beneath a layer of fear, of doubt.

And Ethan knew this—he couldn't lose her. Not now.

Not when she was so close to breaking.

Ten

Fractured Foundations

The next few days passed in a blur of half-hearted effort and fleeting moments of tension. Sienna's Brew remained open, its doors unlocked, but the life in the café had started to wither. Sienna, as always, did her best to keep up appearances—working the counter, greeting the occasional customer with a smile, making lattes and cappuccinos with the precision she had honed over the years. But Ethan could see it in her eyes—something had shifted. A heaviness lingered in her expression, and it weighed on him too.

He kept waiting for the moment when she would crack, for the time when the dam would break and she would let herself lean on someone, let herself admit that it wasn't just the café at stake here. But that moment never came. Instead, she locked herself away even more, throwing herself into the daily grind like it was the only thing keeping her from falling apart.

Ethan, too, found himself lost in the motions. He spent hours cleaning, brewing, trying his best to fill the space between them with small talk and light conversation, but it never worked. Sienna had pulled away, retreating into herself again, her walls as high as they had ever been.

The café had started to feel like a ghost town—quiet, lifeless, filled with memories of what it had been. The customers had stopped coming as often, and with the looming threat of Perrault's takeover, the energy had drained from the room.

It wasn't until late one night, as Ethan was finishing up the last of the cleaning, that he finally caught her.

She was sitting in the far corner of the café, her elbows resting on the table, her head bent low, her fingers sifting through a pile of papers. The dim light cast shadows across her face, but it didn't mask the exhaustion written all over her. It wasn't just physical weariness—it was defeat.

Ethan couldn't stand it any longer.

He set the rag down, his footsteps barely audible against the wooden floor as he walked toward her. The distant sound of a passing car's tires on wet pavement was the only thing that broke the silence between them.

"Sienna?" he said, his voice soft but insistent.

She didn't look up immediately, but after a long pause, she raised her head, her eyes locking with his. For a moment, the world seemed to hold its breath. Then, without a word, she dropped her gaze back down to the papers.

"What are you doing?" he asked, stepping closer.

"Just… checking the numbers," she said, her voice tired, strained. "Seeing how much longer I can keep this place running."

The words hit him like a punch to the gut, but he didn't let it show. Instead, he crouched down beside her, his gaze flicking to the mess of invoices and rent notices scattered across the table.

"Sienna, you can't keep going like this," he said, his voice firm but gentle. "You're killing yourself over this place. You're pushing yourself to the breaking point. And I'm watching you slip through my fingers. We're all watching."

Her eyes flicked up to his, a flash of anger sparking behind her tired gaze. "What do you want from me, Ethan?" she asked, her voice sharp. "What do you want me to say? That I'm done? That I'm ready to throw in the towel and walk away? Because that's what you're hoping for, isn't it? That I'll just give up and let you be the hero in all of this. Let you swoop in and save me." She stood up abruptly, the chair scraping against the floor as she backed away from him. "But it's not that easy. You don't understand."

Ethan's breath caught in his throat. Her words cut deep, but they also rang with the truth. She was right. He didn't understand everything. He didn't know what it felt like to lose everything you'd worked for. He didn't know what it felt like to have your world crumble around you and be powerless to stop it.

"I don't need saving, Ethan," Sienna continued, her voice trembling now, the anger fading into frustration. "I've been doing this on my own for years. I've made it this far without anyone's help. And now you're here, trying to fix everything. But you can't fix this. Nothing can fix this."

The bitterness in her voice stung, but it was the fear beneath it that twisted in his gut. He knew that fear. He'd seen it in himself, too many times. That crippling, paralyzing fear that everything you've built is fragile, that it could all fall apart at any moment. And once it's gone, you can't get it back.

Ethan rose to his feet slowly, his mind racing. "I'm not trying to fix it for you, Sienna," he said, his voice low. "But I'm here. And I'm not going anywhere. You don't have to do this alone."

She turned away from him, her back stiff. "I've been alone for a long time. I don't need anyone else to see me fall apart."

Ethan took a step closer, his voice softening, but his words more urgent. "You're not alone, Sienna. Not anymore."

She remained silent for a moment, and for a second, he thought she might walk away again. But instead, she let out a shaky breath and turned back toward him, her eyes filled with something he couldn't name—vulnerability.

"Then what do you want me to do, Ethan?" Her voice cracked. "What am I supposed to do when everything is crumbling around me? When I can't keep up the fight anymore? Do you want me to just roll over and let Perrault win? Is that what you want?"

Ethan reached for her, his hand resting on her arm, steadying her as she shook with frustration and fear. His chest tightened, a mixture of anger and helplessness surging through him. "No, Sienna. I want you to keep fighting. But not alone. Not like this. We fight together. You don't have to carry this weight by yourself anymore."

For a long moment, they stood there, the world outside the café slipping away. Sienna's breathing slowed, the tension in her shoulders easing just slightly as Ethan's words hung in the air between them.

Then, she spoke again, her voice barely above a whisper. "I don't know how much longer I can do this."

"I know," Ethan replied quietly. "But I'm not going anywhere. And I'm not going to let you give up."

Her eyes met his, searching his face, trying to find the truth behind his words. "What if I can't win, Ethan? What if I've already lost?"

Ethan's heart hammered in his chest. This was it—the moment he knew had been coming. The moment when the reality of everything she had been hiding from would catch up to her, and she would finally have to face it.

"Then we'll fight until we can't fight anymore," he said firmly. "And when it's all over, we'll figure out what comes next. Together."

Sienna's eyes softened slightly, the first hint of trust slipping through the cracks in her walls. But just as she was about to speak again, the door to the café opened, the harsh jingle of the bell cutting through the air.

Ethan's heart sank as he saw who was standing in the doorway.

It was Julian Marks.

He walked into the café like he owned it, his cold gaze flicking over Ethan before settling on Sienna.

"Did I interrupt something?" Julian asked, his voice smooth, casual, but there was an unmistakable edge to it.

Sienna's entire body stiffened, and Ethan could see the fear creeping back into her expression. This wasn't just another business meeting. This was a confrontation. A showdown.

Julian stepped forward, unfazed by the tension in the room. "I came to deliver a message. I think you've made your point, Sienna. But it's time to stop pretending this little café can survive. It's over."

Ethan took a step forward, positioning himself slightly in front of Sienna. "You're wrong, Julian. It's not over. And I'm not going to let you destroy everything she's worked for."

Julian's smile widened, but it didn't reach his eyes. "We'll see about that," he said, his tone dripping with menace.

Sienna's gaze flicked to Ethan, her eyes filled with something different now—resolve. She wasn't backing down. Not this time.

"We're just getting started," she said, her voice steady. "And you're not going to stop me."

Julian's smile faltered for just a moment, but it was enough. Ethan knew it. This fight wasn't over yet.

Eleven

Glimmer of Hope

The night air outside had grown thick with tension, like the calm before a storm. The usual hum of the city, distant and faint, felt like it was holding its breath as Ethan stood across from Julian Marks, watching him with a cool detachment that masked the growing heat in his chest. Sienna stood beside him, her posture rigid, her eyes narrowed—she was not going to back down. Neither was he.

Julian's presence was like a dark cloud hanging over them, his expensive suit and polished demeanor everything Ethan had come to expect from the corporate world—a world that was so different from the humble warmth of Sienna's Brew, a place that had weathered storms far greater than this one.

Julian looked between them, his lips curling into that too-perfect smile. "You two think this is some kind of stand-off, don't you?" he said, his voice dripping with condescension. "But you're wasting your time. I don't need to 'take you down,' Sienna. You're already crumbling. The numbers don't lie."

Sienna's eyes flashed. "I told you, I'm not selling."

Julian's smile didn't falter. "You might not have a choice. Perrault's got the capital to crush you. All the lawyers, all the contracts. You can't win this battle."

Sienna took a deep breath, and Ethan watched as she stood a little straighter, her resolve building. She wasn't done yet. Not by a long shot.

"You may have money and power, Julian," she said, her voice steady, "but you don't know what it takes to keep a place like this alive. You think you can buy me out, but you can't buy my heart. This café means more to me than your paycheck ever will."

Julian paused for a moment, studying her with an unreadable expression. Then, with a dramatic sigh, he leaned in slightly, his voice turning colder. "You really think you can survive the corporate storm, Sienna? You think all this heart you've got is going to keep this place running?" He glanced at Ethan, who had been standing quietly beside Sienna, an unwavering presence of support. "What does he know about survival? He's just some hired help."

Ethan's jaw clenched, but he didn't take the bait. He had no interest in fighting Julian's mind games. Instead, he focused on

Sienna, his gaze steady, silently telling her to stay focused.

Sienna's lips pressed into a thin line. Her anger, her frustration—it was all there, just below the surface, but she kept her cool. "You're wrong," she said, her voice quiet but filled with an unshakable conviction. "You think that just because you've got a lot of money, you've won. But you're wrong. You've never understood what it takes to build something real. Something that matters to people. This café is more than just a business, Julian. It's part of this community. It's part of me."

Julian's expression flickered. Just for a second. A crack.

But it was enough for Ethan to see it. He had her. Sienna had made her stand, and there was no going back now.

"You're fighting for a dying cause, Sienna," Julian said, his tone taking on a colder edge. "Perrault doesn't lose. We'll bury this place, and you'll have nothing left. I'll make sure of it."

Sienna didn't flinch. Instead, she met his gaze with fire in her eyes. "You can't destroy what's already been built. Not without breaking every single person who believes in it." She looked at Ethan now, her voice softer but resolute. "And that includes me."

For the first time, Julian seemed to hesitate. His eyes flickered to Ethan, then back to Sienna, but his smirk didn't return. He straightened up, his posture stiffening.

"This is your last chance, Sienna," he said, his voice taking on an almost threatening tone. "Take the offer. Or I'll make sure this café is gone by the end of the month."

Sienna didn't even blink. "Then you can consider this my final refusal. Get out, Julian." Her voice, though calm, held such finality that it could have frozen anyone in place.

Julian's eyes darkened, but after a long, tense moment, he let out a low chuckle. "Very well. But don't say I didn't warn you." His gaze lingered on Sienna, a challenge hidden beneath the surface, before he turned and walked out of the café, the door swinging closed behind him with a sharp, final click.

The instant he was gone, the weight in the room seemed to shift. The silence that followed was deafening.

Ethan didn't know what to say, so he said nothing. He simply stood there, watching Sienna. The café felt different now. Lighter. But there was a nervous energy in the air, a storm still brewing.

Sienna stood for a long moment, her back to Ethan, before slowly turning to face him. Her expression was unreadable, but Ethan could see the tension in her shoulders, the way her hands were trembling slightly at her sides.

"You did it," he said, his voice quiet but filled with admiration. "You stood your ground."

She looked at him then, her eyes filled with exhaustion, but also something else—gratitude. "I couldn't just let him push me around," she said, her voice low. "I've been fighting this battle for too long to give up now."

Ethan took a step closer. "I know you have. But you don't have to fight it alone anymore." He paused for a moment, watching her carefully. "I'm not going anywhere, Sienna. I'm here. And I'm not going to let you lose this place."

She didn't speak immediately, just stood there, as if weighing his words. Then, her gaze softened, and she gave a small, weary smile. "You don't know what this means to me, Ethan. I… I never thought anyone would understand what it's like to keep something like this alive. To have everything riding on it."

"I get it," he said, his voice sincere. "I might not have built it, but I see how much it matters. And I'm not giving up on you."

For a moment, the weight of everything seemed to settle between them. The anger from Julian's visit, the pressure of the looming threat, the uncertainty that had been gnawing at Sienna—it all seemed to melt away, replaced by something warm, something hopeful.

Sienna took a deep breath and let it out slowly. "I don't know what's going to happen next. But for the first time in a long time, I think… I think we've got a shot."

Ethan smiled, the tension lifting from his chest for the first time in days. "We're not done yet. We've still got a fight to win."

Sienna's gaze lingered on him, her eyes softening. "Thank you," she said, her voice almost too quiet to hear. "For everything."

Ethan nodded, but before he could say anything more, his phone buzzed in his pocket. He pulled it out quickly, checking the message. His stomach dropped as he read the text.

It was from Claire.

"The offer from Perrault came through. They've matched the buyout price, and the contract's waiting for your signature. I don't know how much longer we can hold them off. You need to make a decision soon."

Ethan's mind raced, his heart pounding in his chest. This was it. The moment he had been dreading. Sienna had just stood her ground, and now it was time for him to decide. Was he going to honor the promise he'd made to her, or was he going to betray everything they'd fought for?

He looked up at Sienna, her face still soft with the relief of the moment. She didn't know the full extent of what was happening behind the scenes. She didn't know that the stakes were higher than just her café. They were higher than his job. Higher than anything.

He had to make a choice. And soon.

Sienna was waiting for him to speak, her eyes still filled with the hope he'd given her. But in the back of his mind, Ethan felt the weight of the decision he was about to make. Would he stand by her, or would he become another piece in Perrault's corporate machine?

The choice was his.

Twelve

The Choice

The hours stretched long into the night, and the quiet of Sienna's Brew felt more suffocating than ever. The café, once full of the constant hum of conversation and the clinking of cups and spoons, now sat in eerie silence. Even the buzz of the refrigerators had quieted, as though the place itself were holding its breath, waiting for the storm that had been building on the horizon to finally break.

Ethan's mind raced. The message. The decision. He could feel the weight of Claire's text pressing down on him, pulling at his every thought, forcing his focus onto one thing: the offer from Perrault. The money, the buyout, the chance to walk away from all of this without losing everything. It could solve everything.

But there was something else that gnawed at him, something deep in his chest that refused to let go.

He wasn't just fighting for a business—he was fighting for a person. For Sienna.

She was standing by the window now, looking out into the night, her arms crossed tightly over her chest, the faintest tremor in her fingers. Ethan couldn't remember the last time she'd let herself breathe, let alone relax. Everything she did was for the café, for the fight that never seemed to end, and now, after Julian's threats and the constant pressure from Perrault, she was standing at the edge of something much darker than even she realized.

The tension between them had been mounting for days. Every word that passed between them felt more like a challenge, a question that neither one of them could answer. They were both running out of time, and the weight of it had become unbearable.

"Are you going to keep standing there, or are you going to talk to me?" Sienna's voice was quiet but sharp, the edge of frustration evident in her tone. She hadn't turned around, but she didn't need to. Ethan could feel her eyes on him, even from behind.

"I was just… thinking," he said, though the words felt hollow.

"You always seem to be thinking these days," she replied, her voice colder now. She finally turned to face him, her expression unreadable. "What's going on, Ethan? You've been quiet. Too quiet."

Ethan hesitated. The decision was gnawing at him. His loyalty

The Choice

to Sienna, to this place, to everything she'd built—how could he possibly walk away from that? But the text from Claire was right in front of him, the offer from Perrault's lawyers staring back at him like an escape route.

"I got a message," he finally said, his voice tight with the weight of it. "From Claire. The buyout offer from Perrault has been matched. They're offering the exact amount. It's all in place, waiting for my signature."

Sienna's gaze didn't waver. Her body stiffened ever so slightly, but she didn't move.

"So that's it, then?" she asked, her voice barely a whisper. "You're just going to sell me out?"

Ethan flinched, the words cutting deeper than he expected. But he held his ground. "I'm not selling you out. I'm trying to figure out if this is worth it. If this place is worth losing everything else."

She blinked, her expression softening, but only slightly. "What do you mean, losing everything else?"

Ethan took a deep breath, stepping closer to her. "Perrault's offer isn't just for the café. It's for me, too. I don't know if you realized, but they've been keeping track of me, Sienna. I'm not just some guy off the street. I'm a part of all of this now. If I don't sign, they'll use me against you. And I don't know how much longer I can keep playing this game."

Sienna's face twisted in disbelief. "You think they'll use you?" Her voice was sharp with a bitter laugh. "You think they'll just throw you away when you're not useful anymore?"

Ethan hesitated. "I think they'll stop at nothing to get what they want. And if I don't help them, they'll turn on me. And you."

Sienna's eyes darkened. "I don't need your help, Ethan. I don't need you to fight my battles for me. I've been doing this alone for too long to let anyone walk in and take over."

"I'm not trying to take over," he said, his voice thick with frustration. "I'm trying to help you, Sienna. I'm trying to keep you from getting destroyed by these people. But you're making it impossible. You're pushing everyone away."

Sienna took a step back, her face softening just a little, but her words were still cold. "Maybe I don't want your help," she said, her eyes flashing. "Maybe I don't need anyone to come in and save me from myself."

"Save you?" Ethan repeated, his voice rising slightly. "I'm not here to save you. I'm here to help you keep your dreams alive, Sienna! But you're pushing me away."

She stood there for a moment, her hands trembling at her sides. "And you think I can just let you in? Just because you say so?" she asked, her voice trembling with anger. "You don't understand how much I've sacrificed for this place. You don't know how many times I've been told to walk away, to sell, to give up. And every single time, I've stood my ground. I've kept this place alive with nothing but my own hands. And you think that now, after everything, I'm just going to let you fix it all? You think I'm just going to let you write the ending?"

Ethan stepped forward, feeling his heart pounding in his chest. "No," he said, his voice firm now. "I don't think I can fix everything. But I'm willing to try. I'm willing to fight. And I'll do whatever it takes to make sure you don't lose it all."

Sienna's eyes burned into him. The anger was still there, but so was something else—something vulnerable, something that Ethan hadn't seen before. She opened her mouth to speak, but the words died in her throat.

"I'm not like you, Ethan," she said softly, her voice breaking. "I don't know how to let people in. I don't know how to trust anyone with this… with me."

Ethan reached out, his hand gently touching her arm, his fingers trembling. He could see the walls she'd built around herself—walls that had kept her safe from the world, but had also kept her isolated, alone.

"You don't have to do this alone, Sienna," he said softly, his voice steady but filled with a quiet urgency. "I'm here. And I'm not going anywhere."

For a long moment, Sienna said nothing. She didn't pull away from his touch, but she didn't lean into it either. There was something between them—something unspoken, something fragile.

The Silent Investor

And then, at last, she spoke.

"You don't know what this place means to me," she said, her voice barely above a whisper. "It's not just a business. It's everything. It's… it's the only thing I've ever had that's been mine. And I'm so afraid to lose it, Ethan. So afraid that I'm going to lose everything."

Ethan swallowed hard, his heart aching for her. The vulnerability in her words hit him harder than he expected. She wasn't just scared for the café. She was scared of losing herself in the process.

"You won't lose it," he said, his voice low but steady. "Not if I have anything to say about it."

Sienna looked up at him then, her eyes filled with a mixture of hope and disbelief. "You'd fight for me?" she asked, her voice wavering.

"Always," he replied, his hand still resting on her arm.

For a moment, Sienna didn't say anything. Then, slowly, she nodded, her lips parting as if to speak—but the words caught in her throat. Finally, she whispered, "Then what do we do now?"

Ethan took a deep breath, pulling back slightly but keeping his hand on her arm. He glanced down at the phone in his pocket, the message from Claire still fresh in his mind, the contract from Perrault still waiting to be signed.

The Choice

"I don't know yet," he said quietly. "But whatever happens… we'll face it together."

Sienna looked at him, her eyes searching his, and for the first time in what felt like forever, a flicker of something hopeful passed between them.

She didn't say anything more. She didn't need to.

The fight wasn't over. Not by a long shot.

And this time, they would fight together.

Thirteen

Last Stand

The days that followed were filled with a sense of urgency—of tension that clung to every corner of Sienna's Brew, thick enough to suffocate.

Sienna had been quiet since their conversation, quieter than usual, and even though Ethan had kept his promise to stay by her side, the weight of the looming decision hung heavy between them. The walls she'd built around herself were still up, though she no longer avoided his presence. Every so often, their eyes would meet, a silent understanding passing between them. But Sienna was still too afraid to let go, too afraid to believe that maybe, just maybe, things could change.

The café had emptied out earlier than usual that night. A handful of regulars had come and gone, most of them offering their usual smiles and pleasantries, but none of them lingered.

Last Stand

The energy that once filled this place—the energy that had once seemed endless—had become a fragile thing, barely held together by the thin threads of hope and determination that Sienna clung to. Even the espresso machine, which had been the heartbeat of this café, now felt like a distant echo, its hisses and whirs fading into the background.

Sienna stood behind the counter, the familiar routine of cleaning and organizing offering her no real relief. The papers were still there, scattered across the countertop—lease agreements, supplier invoices, and the ever-present buyout offer from Perrault. But tonight, it wasn't the paperwork that consumed her; it was the crushing realization that the end was near. She couldn't run from it anymore. She could feel the walls closing in.

Ethan had spent the last few hours cleaning the café with mechanical precision. He wiped down counters, cleaned the windows, checked inventory—anything to keep his mind busy, anything to avoid confronting the reality that was starting to set in. But now, as the café grew darker with each passing minute, Ethan couldn't escape the gnawing feeling in his chest.

They were running out of time. And neither of them knew what came next.

As he wiped down the counter, his phone buzzed in his pocket. It was Claire again, her message brief but clear:

"Perrault's offer expires in two days. They won't extend it. You need to make a decision."

His gut twisted as he read the words again, and for the first time in days, his focus broke. The weight of the decision he was facing came crashing back with full force. He needed to make a choice.

"Is everything okay?" Sienna's voice broke through his thoughts, and he looked up to find her watching him closely, her expression unreadable. The tension between them had become palpable.

Ethan hesitated, his mind still racing. He couldn't lie to her—not now. He couldn't pretend everything was fine when it wasn't. But at the same time, he didn't want to add to her already overwhelming burden.

"I just got a message," he said quietly, trying to keep his voice steady. "The buyout offer from Perrault expires in two days. Claire says they won't extend it."

Sienna's face hardened, the familiar walls rising again as she stepped back from the counter. She crossed her arms tightly, her jaw setting in that stubborn way he'd come to recognize. "So it's finally come down to it, hasn't it?" Her voice was cold now, a deliberate distance between them.

Ethan sighed, stepping closer, his own frustration building. "Sienna, I don't want to do this. But they've been pressuring me for months now. And if I don't sign, if I don't help them finalize this, they'll turn everything against you—against us." His voice faltered for just a moment, the weight of the choice making his stomach churn. "I don't know how much longer I can keep fighting them, not with the way they've set things up."

Sienna's eyes flashed with anger, and for a moment, Ethan was afraid she might lash out. But instead, she simply stared at him, the hurt in her eyes sharper than any words she could've said. "So you're telling me that after everything, after all the promises, after all the times you told me you wouldn't leave, you're just going to sell me out?"

Ethan flinched, the words stinging. "I'm not selling you out, Sienna. I'm trying to protect you."

"By doing exactly what they want?" she shot back, her voice rising. "That's not protecting me, Ethan. That's betraying me. It's everything I've fought against—everything I've worked for. You can't just walk in here and tell me what to do. You're not the one who's going to lose everything."

The sharpness in her voice cut through him like a blade, and for the first time, he felt the full weight of their differences. She had been fighting this battle alone for so long that it seemed impossible to her that anyone could understand. And yet, he had tried to—he had tried to be there for her, to support her, to keep the fight alive. But now… now he was beginning to feel like they were at the edge of a cliff, with nowhere left to go but down.

"I don't know what else to do," Ethan said, his voice strained, the helplessness creeping in. "You're right. I'm not the one who's going to lose everything. I'm not the one who built this place. But I can't stand by and watch you lose it. You can't keep fighting alone, Sienna. You have to make a choice too."

Her eyes flickered with something—fear, maybe, or uncertainty—but she didn't respond. Instead, she turned away, her back to him as she stared out the window. The cold light of the streetlamps spilled across the café, casting long shadows in every corner. Ethan watched her, feeling more helpless than ever. He wanted to reach out, to pull her back, but he didn't know how. Didn't know if she would even let him.

For a long time, neither of them spoke. The silence between them was suffocating, as thick as the storm clouds that had gathered outside. Ethan could feel his own anger, his frustration rising, but he didn't know how to break through.

And then, as though the tension in the room had finally broken, Sienna spoke. Her voice was quiet, almost to the point of breaking. "I can't just give up, Ethan. I've spent everything I have on this place. I've given everything." Her hands trembled as she turned around, her face softening, her voice barely above a whisper. "I can't let them take it away from me. I can't let Perrault win."

Ethan's heart clenched. She wasn't giving up. She couldn't. She was stronger than that. He stepped forward, his hand reaching for hers, the warmth of her skin sending a jolt of electricity through him.

"You don't have to fight alone anymore, Sienna," he said softly. "You never did. We'll find another way. We'll figure it out together."

Sienna stared at him for a long moment, her eyes searching his, as if trying to find the truth in his words. Finally, she nodded, her fingers curling around his.

"Then we fight," she whispered, her voice steady now. "But this time, we do it my way."

The weight of that decision hung between them, a turning point they couldn't undo. Ethan felt a surge of relief flood through him. She was still in the fight, and for the first time, they were in it together.

But the storm wasn't over. In fact, it was just beginning.

As they stood there, hands clasped, the door to the café swung open once again, the familiar chime ringing through the stillness. But this time, it wasn't Julian Marks. It was someone else—someone with a face Ethan didn't recognize. The man stepped inside with an air of purpose, his eyes scanning the café as though he owned the place. He didn't look like a customer. He looked like someone who had come for something else.

"Can I help you?" Sienna asked, her voice steady despite the tension still hanging in the air.

The man's eyes flicked to her, then to Ethan, before he spoke. "I'm here on behalf of Perrault Coffee," he said smoothly. "And I think it's time we finally have a serious conversation about your future."

Ethan's pulse quickened. This wasn't over.

The man's presence, his very words, felt like the first crack of thunder before the storm unleashed its fury. The fight for Sienna's Brew was far from over.

Fourteen

The Breaking Point

The moment the door swung open, Sienna felt it—the same electric shock of tension that had been building for days. The man who stepped inside wasn't like the others. His presence was different, colder, like a shadow that stretched across the room and refused to leave.

Ethan stepped closer, his body instinctively moving to shield her. He wasn't sure why he was so protective—maybe it was because he saw the cracks in her armor, the raw vulnerability that had been exposed in their earlier conversations. Or maybe it was because he knew, deep down, that this was the moment when everything would either fall apart or somehow—miraculously—hold together.

The man didn't even look at him as he entered, his eyes immediately locking onto Sienna. He was tall, wearing a dark suit, his expression impassive, yet there was an air of arrogance about him—one that reeked of corporate power and entitlement. He was here for something. Ethan could feel it.

Sienna stood frozen behind the counter, her hand gripping the edge of the counter so tightly that her knuckles were white. Ethan could see it—the way she braced herself, the flicker of fear in her eyes. She hadn't been expecting this kind of confrontation. But then again, after everything that had happened, neither had he.

"I don't believe we've met," Sienna said, her voice cool and controlled, but there was a sharp edge to it. She wasn't going to back down now. She was stronger than that. Ethan could see it in the way she held herself.

The man smiled faintly, but there was no warmth in it. "You're Sienna Carter, aren't you?" he asked, his tone casual, almost dismissive. "I was hoping to speak with you about your café."

Ethan stepped forward, his voice firm. "And who are you?"

The man turned his gaze to him, his eyes briefly flicking over Ethan as if he were nothing more than a nuisance. "I'm here on behalf of Perrault Coffee. My name is Henry Davis." His voice was smooth, calculated, like the kind of voice someone would use when delivering bad news with a smile. "And I believe it's time we discussed your future."

Sienna's body tensed beside Ethan, and he could feel her pulse quicken. She wasn't buying this man's charm for a second, and neither was he.

"Is that so?" Sienna's voice had dropped, becoming colder, sharper. "And why would I want to discuss anything with Perrault Coffee?"

Henry's smile didn't falter, but his eyes grew darker, more intent. "Let's not pretend you don't know why I'm here, Sienna. Your café is a failing business. The foot traffic is dwindling, your revenue is in a downward spiral. Perrault could save you from losing everything. Or you could fight a losing battle and watch it all fall apart. The choice is simple."

Ethan felt the anger flare in his chest, but he didn't interrupt. He couldn't afford to. Not yet. Not until he understood what was really happening.

Sienna's eyes narrowed, her jaw tightening. "I'm not selling. Not to you, not to anyone."

Henry's gaze flickered to Ethan for a moment before returning to Sienna. "Stubbornness will get you nowhere. Your pride will be the death of this café. But I'm not here to argue with you about that. I'm here to offer you a way out."

Sienna's lips curled into a bitter smile. "You're trying to buy me out again. But it's not going to work this time, Henry. I've already said no."

The man's eyes darkened, and Ethan felt an ominous shift in the air. Henry's calm demeanor had shifted slightly, replaced with something more aggressive. "You think you can keep this place running on pride alone? You're delusional, Sienna. Perrault is offering you a chance to leave with dignity. All you have to do is sign. You walk away with the money you need, and we take care of the rest. You'll never have to worry about this place again."

Sienna stood her ground, her eyes burning with an intensity that made Ethan's chest tighten. "I'll never sell to Perrault. Not when I've spent years building this place from the ground up. Not when it's my café. You don't get to decide when it's over."

Henry's smile vanished, replaced by something far colder, far more calculating. He took a step forward, his presence suddenly overpowering, looming over them both. Ethan's instincts screamed at him to move, but he didn't. He couldn't. He wasn't about to back down, not with Sienna so close to losing everything she cared about.

"Don't make this harder than it needs to be, Sienna," Henry said, his voice low, dangerous. "I'm here because Perrault wants this café. And if you refuse to sell, I'll make sure you lose it one way or another. It doesn't matter how much you fight. It doesn't matter how much you cling to it. If you don't sign, you'll have nothing left."

Sienna flinched slightly, but only for a moment. The fear in her eyes wasn't enough to make her crumble. Instead, she stood taller, her gaze unwavering. "You can't take something that's already mine. You can't destroy it."

The Breaking Point

Henry laughed, but it wasn't a laugh of amusement. It was a laugh that held a deeper, darker meaning—one that made the air feel colder. "That's where you're wrong, Sienna. Everything is for sale, even your pride. And Perrault always gets what it wants."

Ethan's mind raced. This was it. The breaking point. He could see it now—Perrault had no intention of negotiating. They didn't care about fair play or compromises. They wanted it all, and they were willing to destroy whatever stood in their way to get it.

And that included her.

Sienna's body was tense, but her voice was steady as she met Henry's gaze. "You'll have to do more than scare me to get what you want."

Henry raised an eyebrow, his expression unamused. "Is that so? I'm afraid you don't have much of a choice in the matter." He took a step back, pulling a folded piece of paper from his jacket pocket. He slapped it down onto the counter between them, his gaze never leaving Sienna's face. "This is your final offer. Sign it, and we'll take care of everything. Walk away, and we'll make sure this café closes its doors for good. No more delays. No more back-and-forth."

The room seemed to hold its breath. The silence was deafening. Ethan looked at the paper, but he couldn't bring himself to reach for it. He didn't need to see it. He already knew what it said.

Sienna didn't move. She didn't even look at the paper. Instead, her eyes remained locked on Henry's, the fire in her gaze stronger than ever.

"You think I'm afraid of you?" she said, her voice almost a whisper, but cutting through the air like a blade. "You think that after everything I've been through, after everything I've lost, that I'm going to roll over and sell out to a corporation that doesn't care about anything but profit?"

Henry's face remained impassive, but there was a flicker of annoyance in his eyes. "You're wasting your time, Sienna. You're only delaying the inevitable. This is your last chance."

For a long moment, neither of them spoke. Ethan could feel the tension between them, thick and heavy, a battle of wills that could end in only one way. He watched Sienna closely, her fingers twitching slightly at her sides, the weight of the decision pressing down on her.

Then, with a slow, deliberate movement, she reached for the paper. Her fingers brushed against it for a moment, as if she were testing it, feeling the finality of the moment. And then, without another word, she ripped it in half.

The sound was sharp—loud enough to break through the suffocating silence.

Henry's eyes narrowed, his lips curling into a dangerous smile. "You've made a grave mistake," he said, his voice cold, but there was a flicker of something else—frustration. "But don't think this is over, Sienna. You've made an enemy today, and there's no going back from that."

Sienna didn't flinch. She didn't look at him as he turned and walked out, the door slamming behind him with a finality that echoed in the hollow space.

Ethan stood frozen, watching her. He wasn't sure what had just happened, but he knew this: Sienna had just chosen her fate.

She had chosen to fight.

Fifteen

Consequence of Choice

The door clicked shut behind Henry with a finality that rang through the room. Sienna stood motionless for a few seconds, her back turned to Ethan, staring at the space where the man had just been, his threat lingering in the air like smoke. Ethan could feel the tension in her, the way her body was holding tight, as if bracing for something to break. But what exactly? What had Henry's words done to her?

For a moment, neither of them moved.

Then, Sienna spoke, her voice low, almost mechanical. "I'm not going to let them take it."

Ethan didn't know if she was speaking to him, to herself, or to the world. But he knew this wasn't over. Her decision, ripping up that contract, was the spark that would set everything on fire. This was no longer about a café. This was about who she was and how far she was willing to go to protect it.

"You're not going to let them take it," he repeated quietly, stepping closer to her. "But that means something, Sienna. You know it means something big."

She turned slowly, finally meeting his eyes. There was fire in her gaze now, a fierce resolve that had been buried under the pressure of months of struggle. But underneath the fire, there was something else. Something deeper. Fear.

"I don't care what it takes anymore," she said, the words coming out fast and desperate. "I've lost everything else. I can't let them have this. This café… it's everything I have. I can't just walk away from it, Ethan. I won't."

Ethan's heart twisted at the intensity of her words. It was the truth, raw and unfiltered. But he could see something in her, too. Something that wasn't just about saving the café anymore. This wasn't just about pride. This wasn't about her love for the place. It was about the need to keep control, to stand her ground, to not give in to the overwhelming forces bearing down on her.

"Listen to me," Ethan said, taking another step closer, his voice softening, "I understand. You're not alone in this, Sienna. You don't have to fight alone."

But Sienna's eyes were clouded with something that made him hesitate—doubt. She shook her head, her fists clenched at her sides.

"You don't understand, Ethan. You have no idea what this feels like, what it's like to lose everything you've worked for." Her voice was rising now, the fear spilling out. "You think you can just stand there and tell me it's going to be okay, but you have no idea how deep this goes. You think this is just about a café? This is my life, Ethan. This is all I have left. I can't let it slip away."

Ethan swallowed hard, feeling the weight of her words press against his chest. He could see how much this meant to her, how tightly she was holding on to what little was left. And the truth hit him harder than he expected. She wasn't just protecting a business. She was protecting herself.

But the question still lingered in his mind: How far would she go to keep it?

"Tell me what you need, Sienna," Ethan said, his voice almost a whisper now. "Tell me what I can do."

Sienna's eyes flickered for a moment, uncertainty flashing behind them before she quickly masked it with more defiance. "You don't get it," she repeated, her voice hardening again. "There's nothing anyone can do. I'm done waiting for some miracle. Perrault will destroy this place if I don't act fast enough, and I'm not going to give them that satisfaction."

The fire in her eyes was blazing again, but this time, Ethan could see the cracks in it. The desperation was leaking through.

He stepped forward, his hand gently touching her arm. "You're not alone. You don't have to do this all by yourself."

Sienna pulled away from him, her jaw tight. "I've always done it alone, Ethan. That's how it's always been. Don't you get it? There's no one else who understands what this means. No one else who understands what it's like to fight for something until there's nothing left of you. I've lost my family, I've lost my savings, I've lost... everything. This is all I have left."

Ethan's chest tightened. He understood more than she realized. In his own way, he knew what it felt like to feel like you were drowning and have no one to throw you a rope. But he couldn't let her see that now. He couldn't let her fall deeper into this spiral of fear. He wouldn't let her be swallowed whole.

"We're not talking about a losing battle anymore," Ethan said, his voice steady now. "This is about standing together and making sure Perrault doesn't get what they want. I'll help you, Sienna. We'll do this together."

For a brief moment, Sienna didn't respond. She stood there, her back straight, her shoulders tight as if she was calculating every word, every move. And for the first time, Ethan saw something flicker in her eyes. Something that was both terrifying and beautiful. Hope.

But before either of them could speak again, the bell above the door rang, cutting through the air like a knife.

Sienna froze, her breath catching in her throat, her eyes wide with a mix of fear and fury.

Ethan's body went rigid, his eyes darting toward the entrance. The man who walked in this time wasn't just anyone. He wasn't Henry or Julian. This man was different.

Graham Hunter.

The senior partner at Perrault Coffee—the man who had been the real mastermind behind the company's buyout tactics. Ethan recognized him immediately. Graham had been at the center of every push to break Sienna's resolve. The man was cold, calculated, a predator in every sense of the word.

And he was here to make sure Sienna's decision wasn't hers to make anymore.

"Good evening, Ms. Carter," Graham's voice was smooth, but the edge of menace underneath made Ethan's blood run cold. "I've been expecting you to make the right choice."

Sienna's eyes narrowed, and Ethan could see the muscles in her body tighten, every instinct on alert. She wasn't backing down now—not to him. Not to anyone.

"I've already made my choice," she said, her voice steady, but the tremor was still there beneath it, the fear of what was coming next. "I'm not selling."

Graham's lips twitched into a smile that didn't reach his eyes. "I think you'll find that you don't have much of a choice. I came to deliver the final offer, Sienna. And to remind you that it's not just about you anymore. It's about the people who depend on you. You're running out of time."

Ethan could see it in her eyes now—the doubt that she'd been trying so hard to suppress. She wasn't just fighting for the café anymore. She was fighting for herself, for something deeper that she couldn't explain.

"I've told you no." Sienna's voice was cold now, cutting through the air like steel. She was standing her ground. "You can take your final offer and leave. It's not happening."

Graham's expression darkened, his smile faltering just slightly. The air around them shifted, and Ethan could feel the tension crackling between them like static before a thunderstorm. This wasn't just a business negotiation anymore. This was a battle for control, and Sienna had just declared war.

"I'll give you one last chance to reconsider," Graham said, his voice no longer smooth, but edged with irritation. "After that, I'm afraid we'll have to handle things the hard way."

Ethan's body tensed. He could feel the storm on the horizon, the impending chaos that was about to erupt. This was no longer about saving Sienna's café. It was about saving her.

"I don't need your offers, Graham," Sienna said, her voice shaking with something that was almost fury. "You're not going to intimidate me. I will not sell to you."

Graham's gaze lingered on her for a moment, as if weighing her resolve. But then, his smile returned, colder this time.

"We'll see," he said, his tone low. "We'll see how long your pride lasts."

With that, he turned on his heel and walked out, the door closing with a click that felt like the sound of a trap being set.

Sienna stood still for a long moment, her hands clenched at her sides. Ethan stepped closer, his heart pounding in his chest. This was it. The final confrontation. There was no more running. No more negotiating.

Sienna had made her stand. And now it was time to fight.

"We do this together," Ethan said softly, his hand finding hers. "No matter what happens next."

Sienna looked at him, her eyes filled with a mix of fear and resolve, but there was a glimmer of something else there too. A hint of hope.

"I'm ready," she whispered.

And together, they would face whatever came next.

Sixteen

Final Hour

The clock on the wall above the counter ticked steadily, each second dragging on like an eternity. It was nearing closing time, but neither Ethan nor Sienna moved to clean the last of the tables. There was no rush to finish, no hurry to close. They were waiting. Waiting for the storm to hit, knowing that they were out of time.

The café, which had once been filled with the soft hum of conversation, the scent of freshly ground coffee, and the laughter of regulars, now stood in unnerving silence. The neon lights outside reflected on the glass window, casting eerie glows onto the empty tables. Every corner of the room felt heavy, filled with the weight of decisions that had been made, promises that had been broken, and the tension of the final hours before everything came crashing down.

Ethan stood by the counter, absently wiping down a cup that didn't need wiping. His mind was elsewhere, torn between the promise he'd made to Sienna and the knowledge that time was running out. He couldn't stand the quiet anymore. The stillness in the air was suffocating.

He glanced over at Sienna. She was staring at the papers scattered across the counter—the same ones that had been there for days, the ones that had caused so much pain. Her hands were trembling slightly as she stared at them, but her face remained an unreadable mask. He'd seen her break down, seen her vulnerable and afraid, but this... this was different. This was resolve. A determination that bordered on desperation.

The door chimed, and both of them froze. Ethan turned, heart pounding.

It wasn't a customer this time.

Standing in the doorway was Julian Marks.

Sienna's jaw tightened, and Ethan could see the way her body stiffened as she locked eyes with him. This wasn't the polite, smooth-talking executive she had seen before. This was the man who had made her life hell, the man who had orchestrated the deal with Perrault and made her the target. Ethan could feel the animosity crackling in the air.

Julian stepped into the café, his posture confident, almost smug. The door clicked shut behind him, and the silence settled once again, but this time, it felt oppressive.

"Julian," Sienna said, her voice cold, but Ethan could hear the edge beneath it. She was trying to mask her emotions, but she wasn't fooling anyone. Not Ethan.

Julian smiled, but there was nothing warm about it. It was a smile designed to unsettle, to remind her who held the power. "Sienna, always a pleasure," he said, his voice smooth and insistent. "I trust you're still considering my offer? Time's running out."

Sienna stood her ground. "You've had my answer."

Julian raised an eyebrow, clearly unfazed by her defiance. "You're being stubborn, but I suppose that's nothing new. You always were the difficult one." He stepped closer to the counter, his eyes flicking over the café with the same detached interest he might show toward a piece of property. "This place..." he paused, his eyes settling on her, "is a dying business. And if you think you can keep up this charade, you're only fooling yourself."

Ethan felt his fists clench at his sides. He couldn't stay silent this time. "You don't get to talk to her like that," he said, his voice low but filled with enough anger to make Julian pause.

Julian's eyes flicked to Ethan, a smirk playing at the corners of his mouth. "Ah, the hired help. Still here, I see. Tell me, Ethan, what's it like, playing hero for a woman who's already lost?" He turned back to Sienna, ignoring Ethan entirely. "You're fighting a battle that's already been decided, Sienna. Perrault's grip is tightening, and you're too proud to admit it."

Sienna's face hardened, and Ethan could see the fight in her returning. She wasn't backing down. She had already made her decision. She had already chosen to stand tall, even in the face of overwhelming odds.

"You're wrong, Julian," Sienna said, her voice steady, her gaze unwavering. "You've been wrong this whole time. You think you can come in here, tell me I've lost, and I'll just roll over and sell out. But you don't know me, and you don't understand what this place means to me."

Julian's eyes narrowed, and he took another step toward her. "This isn't about what it means to you. It's about the reality of the situation. I'm offering you an escape, Sienna. I'm giving you a way out before you're buried under a mountain of debt and legal trouble. All you have to do is sign. It's over. And you walk away with your dignity intact. There's no shame in that."

"No shame?" Sienna echoed, her voice rising. "There's no dignity in selling out to you and your corporation. There's no honor in letting people like you stomp all over small businesses just because you can."

Ethan could see the tension building in Julian, the way his smug composure began to crack ever so slightly. But it wasn't enough. Not yet.

"I've made my decision," Sienna continued, her voice now filled with a quiet certainty that sent a shiver down Ethan's spine. "I won't sell. Not to you. Not to Perrault. Not to anyone."

Julian's smile faltered for a brief moment, replaced with a dangerous glint in his eyes. "You'll regret this," he said softly, his voice colder now, the threat beneath it unmistakable. "I'll make sure of that."

Sienna didn't flinch. Instead, she met his gaze, her chin held high. "If you think you can intimidate me into giving up, you're wrong. I've already lost everything else, Julian. This café is all I have left, and I'm not going to let you take it from me. So go ahead. Do your worst."

The silence that followed was thick with tension, the kind that made the air feel heavy, suffocating. Julian's eyes burned with anger now, but he didn't speak again. He simply turned on his heel, his footsteps echoing as he walked toward the door.

Before leaving, he paused, his hand on the door handle. "This is your last chance, Sienna," he said, his voice now low and controlled. "I'll be back, and next time, there won't be a choice."

And with that, he stepped out, the door swinging shut behind him with a force that seemed to rattle the entire room. The chime echoed, but it didn't feel like the ringing of a bell—it felt like the death knell of something much larger.

Ethan exhaled slowly, his body still tense from the confrontation. He glanced over at Sienna, who hadn't moved, hadn't spoken, hadn't even flinched. She was standing tall, her hands clenched at her sides. She looked like a warrior preparing for the battle ahead.

Ethan couldn't help but admire her. He had known this wasn't going to be easy, but he hadn't anticipated just how strong she was—how much she was willing to sacrifice to keep what was hers.

"You did good," he said quietly, his voice almost reverent. "You stood your ground."

Sienna didn't respond immediately. She just stood there, her face unreadable. But after a long moment, she finally turned to him, her eyes softening just slightly. "I don't know how much longer I can keep this up," she said, her voice barely above a whisper. "But I'm not giving up. Not now. Not ever."

Ethan took a step toward her, his hand gently resting on her arm. "You don't have to do this alone, Sienna. You never did. I'm with you."

Sienna looked up at him, her eyes filled with a mix of gratitude and something else—something deeper. "I don't know what's going to happen next. I don't know if I can win."

"We'll find a way," Ethan said, his voice steady. "We'll face it together."

For the first time in days, Sienna gave a small, hesitant smile. It wasn't much, but it was enough. Enough to remind him that there was still hope, that there was still a chance to save this place, to save her.

As they stood there, side by side, the café around them felt

Final Hour

different. Not empty, not hollow, but full of potential—full of the possibility that they could still fight, still win. The final hour was fast approaching, but they weren't out of time yet.

And Sienna wasn't going down without a fight.

Seventeen

Calm Before the Storm

The quiet of the night was like a veil over the city, muffling the usual sounds of the streets, the distant hum of traffic, and the chatter of late-night commuters. Inside Sienna's Brew, the world outside seemed to be a distant memory—frozen, like the moment before a storm. The lights flickered above, casting long shadows over the empty tables, and the smell of coffee, faint but comforting, still lingered in the air, even though the café was now closed.

Sienna stood behind the counter, her fingers lightly grazing the edge of the counter as she stared down at the space in front of her. Ethan stood a few feet away, watching her, knowing that there was something different about the way she held herself now. She wasn't looking at him—not yet—but the silence between them was thick with the weight of everything they had been through. The tension had become a second skin. Both of them knew it was only a matter of time before something would break.

"You can't keep doing this alone, Sienna," Ethan said finally, his voice quiet but firm, like he had been holding the words back for too long. "You've been fighting this battle for months, and I can see it... you're running on fumes."

Sienna didn't answer right away. She kept her gaze fixed on the counter, her face unreadable. The weight of the decision that hung over them both was like an anchor around her neck. The decision to fight back, to refuse the offer from Perrault, to refuse everything she'd worked for. And yet, she didn't know if it was the right choice. How could she?

"I've fought my entire life to keep this place," Sienna finally spoke, her voice barely above a whisper, as if the words themselves were fragile. She didn't look up. "This café is my home. It's everything I've ever built, everything I've ever had. And now... now I have to decide if I'm willing to lose it all." Her voice faltered, just for a second, but it was enough for Ethan to hear the crack in it. The vulnerability that she always tried to hide.

Ethan stepped closer, careful not to invade her space too much, but close enough that she could feel the quiet determination radiating from him. "You don't have to make that decision alone. Not anymore."

Sienna finally turned her head to look at him. Her eyes were bloodshot from sleepless nights and the stress of constant pressure. The look she gave him was one of appreciation and pain—a look that said she was grateful but didn't want to ask for help, didn't want to burden him with her fight. She wanted to keep it all inside, keep it under control.

"You don't understand," she said softly, her words almost lost in the quiet. "I've never had anyone I could trust. Never had anyone who would stand with me when it all came crashing down." Her voice hardened, and the walls she had built around herself began to rise again. "And if I let anyone in now, if I rely on anyone else, what does that make me?"

Ethan could feel the walls rising between them once again. He knew she had been alone for so long, that it was easier for her to keep people at arm's length than to let them in, to trust them. But he couldn't let her shut him out—not now, when the stakes were higher than ever.

"You're not alone, Sienna," he said, his voice firm, his hand reaching out to gently touch hers. "You don't have to do this by yourself anymore. I'm with you. And I'm not going anywhere."

For a long moment, neither of them spoke. The only sound in the café was the distant hum of the streetlights outside, the occasional rustle of paper, the quiet beat of the clock ticking away, as if time itself were moving at a pace that didn't match the gravity of the situation. The moment seemed to stretch on forever, the air thick with unspoken words.

Sienna slowly turned her hand, her fingers brushing against his. Her grip tightened, not quite a hold but a gentle connection, like she was testing it, feeling the steady warmth of his presence. Her eyes softened, but the storm in her gaze hadn't passed. The fight was still there, still alive, but now, it felt like it was for something more.

"I can't lose this," she said quietly, her voice barely audible. "I can't lose everything I've worked for. It's all I have left."

Ethan felt his heart ache for her. He could see the fear in her eyes, the deep, gnawing terror that came with knowing the walls were closing in. He could see how much it hurt her to even think about losing the café, the place she had built from the ground up. But he also saw the spark in her—the thing that refused to die, the thing that was pushing her to fight even when every part of her was exhausted.

"We don't have to lose it," Ethan said softly, but there was a quiet fire in his words. "We'll fight together. This isn't the end. Not for you, not for this café. Not as long as I'm here."

Sienna didn't say anything, but the way her fingers tightened around his gave him the strength he needed. It was a small thing, a simple gesture, but it meant everything. It was the first sign that she wasn't giving up, that she wasn't ready to walk away.

They stood there for what felt like an eternity, locked in that quiet moment, the world outside fading away. The decisions they had to make were still looming, still threatening to tear them apart, but for now, in this moment, it felt like they were holding steady.

And then, just as the quiet seemed to stretch beyond its limits, the door opened again, the familiar chime echoing through the room. Sienna stiffened, her body tensing as if bracing for the worst. Ethan turned toward the door, his hand still resting gently on hers.

The figure that stepped through the door wasn't who they expected. The man who entered was older, in his late fifties, his graying hair slicked back, wearing a sharp, tailored suit. His eyes were cold and calculating, but there was something else in his gaze—something that felt like it belonged in a courtroom or a high-stakes negotiation. This man wasn't here to play games.

Ethan felt his stomach drop.

It was Graham Hunter.

Sienna's breath hitched, her hand sliding away from Ethan's as she stood taller, trying to mask the fear that had crept into her expression. But Ethan could see it—the way her shoulders tightened, the way she squared her jaw as if bracing for the worst.

Graham's cold smile flickered as he took in the scene before him, his eyes lingering on both Sienna and Ethan. "I'm glad to see you've made your decision, Sienna," he said smoothly, his voice dripping with condescension. "But I'm afraid it's too late to change your mind."

Sienna didn't flinch, but Ethan could see the strain on her face, the effort it took to keep her composure. She was done running, done hiding. She was ready to fight.

"I told you before, Graham," Sienna said, her voice cold, "I'm not selling."

Graham stepped forward, his gaze cold and unfaltering. "You don't have a choice. This café is already gone. Perrault has already taken the first step in removing any obstacles. You're not just fighting a losing battle, Sienna. You're fighting a war you can't win. This is the last chance you'll have to walk away with anything. You think you can keep this place open? You think you have the resources? You don't."

The words cut through the air like a blade, and Ethan could feel the weight of them pressing down on him. He had known it would come to this. He had known that Sienna would face something like this—something so much bigger than her, than them. But he wasn't going to let her stand alone. Not now.

Sienna's eyes hardened. "You don't know me, Graham," she said softly, her voice filled with defiance. "And you don't know what I'm willing to fight for. I will not give in. Not now. Not ever."

Graham's smile faltered, but it returned just as quickly, his eyes narrowing in quiet disbelief. "You're making a mistake," he said, almost pityingly. "But it's your choice, Sienna. You'll regret it. You'll see just how far I'm willing to go to make sure you lose."

Ethan felt a surge of anger, his fist tightening, but he held himself in check. This wasn't the time to lose control. Not now, not with everything on the line.

Graham turned to leave, his footsteps echoing through the empty café. "You'll regret this, Sienna," he repeated as the door closed behind him.

Sienna didn't move. She stood there, silent for a moment, the air heavy with the threat of what was to come.

"I won't regret it," she said quietly. Her voice was low, but there was a certainty in it that sent a shiver down Ethan's spine. "Not as long as I'm still standing."

And in that moment, Ethan knew that the battle was just beginning. The storm was coming, and they would face it together. Whatever happened next, they would stand side by side, because she wasn't going down without a fight.

Eighteen

Final Gamble

The night seemed to stretch on forever. The clock ticked, its rhythmic sound echoing through the dimly lit café. Ethan stood across from Sienna, the tension in the air palpable, like the calm before a violent storm. They had both faced down their fears over the past few days, standing their ground against the looming threat of Perrault Coffee, but now, they were standing at the precipice of something much bigger—something far more dangerous.

The doors of Sienna's Brew had been locked for hours now, the café dark and quiet save for the faint hum of the refrigerator. Sienna had barely moved since Graham Hunter left. She had said little, her mind clearly a whirlwind of thoughts, calculations, and doubts. Ethan didn't know what was running through her head, but he could see the strain in her shoulders, the way her fingers were twitching as she absentmindedly fiddled with a napkin at the counter. She was close. Too close.

"Are you okay?" Ethan asked, his voice quiet, hesitant. He had tried to ask her earlier, but she had brushed him off, claiming she was fine. But tonight, something was different. He could see it in her eyes.

Sienna didn't answer immediately. She stared ahead, her jaw tight, her body rigid with the weight of the decision that loomed ahead. Finally, she exhaled slowly and turned to face him. The coldness in her eyes was gone, replaced by something far more uncertain.

"No," she admitted, her voice barely above a whisper. "I'm not okay, Ethan. This has gone too far. I knew it was coming, but now that it's here… I don't know what I'm supposed to do."

Ethan stepped closer, his gaze softening, as he gently placed a hand on her arm. He could feel her tension, the nervous energy radiating from her. "You're not alone in this. I'm not going anywhere."

Sienna shook her head, a bitter laugh escaping her lips. "You keep saying that, Ethan. But it doesn't change anything. It doesn't change the fact that I'm about to lose everything I've built. Everything I've worked for."

Ethan's chest tightened. He knew she was afraid, but this wasn't just fear. This was doubt. The kind of doubt that could break someone, especially someone who had been fighting a battle for as long as she had. He couldn't let her lose that. Not now.

He squeezed her arm gently, his voice steady. "You don't have to lose it. You've already fought too hard. And I'll be damned if I'm going to let you lose it now."

Sienna met his gaze, her eyes searching his, trying to find something—anything—that would tell her that it wasn't over, that they could still turn the tide. The silent battle between them raged in that moment, the weight of their choices settling over both of them.

"I've spent my entire life building this place," she said, her voice cracking. "And now I have to decide if it's worth everything. Worth losing everything. Do I keep fighting for something that might just crush me in the end? Or do I walk away and save myself?"

Ethan didn't flinch. He understood the magnitude of the decision she was facing. But he also knew that she wasn't someone who could just walk away. Not without losing a part of herself. And he wasn't going to let her make that decision alone.

"You don't have to walk away, Sienna," he said firmly. "Not unless you want to. But you don't have to face this alone. Not anymore."

Sienna's fingers twitched again, this time reaching for the paper on the counter—the last of the buyout offers from Perrault. The contract was still there, lying in front of them like a dark promise. A reminder of the only way out they'd been offered. A way to walk away. To let Perrault have it all.

She picked it up slowly, as if testing the weight of it, the feel of it in her hands. Ethan could see her reluctance, the way her fingers hesitated just above the page. He could feel her pulling away, retreating into herself once more.

"I don't know what to do," Sienna said quietly, more to herself than to him. "What if I'm making the wrong choice? What if this is it? What if I've been fighting for something that was doomed from the start?"

Ethan moved around the counter, closing the space between them. His hand brushed against hers, gently guiding the paper from her fingers, his touch lingering just a moment longer than necessary.

"You're not alone in this," he repeated, his voice soft, his presence calm. "And you don't have to make this decision right now. You don't have to carry this weight by yourself."

Sienna glanced at him, her eyes filled with something that felt like desperation. She wanted to believe him, but the fear of everything slipping away was too great. The battle was too real. Everything she had built was slipping from her grasp, and she had no control over it.

"I don't know what's worse," she said, almost to herself. "Losing this place… or letting it be taken from me."

Her voice broke, and for the first time in days, Ethan saw something in her eyes that made his heart ache. Vulnerability. Real vulnerability. The kind that stripped everything bare, the kind that made her human. She wasn't the fierce, unshakable woman she always presented herself to be. She was just a person, a person who had been worn down by the weight of her own fight.

Ethan didn't speak. He didn't need to. His hand found hers, gently but firmly, giving her a steady anchor in the midst of the storm. He wasn't going to let her drown.

And just as they stood there, their hands entwined, the door opened once more.

Sienna's body went rigid again, her eyes snapping toward the door. Ethan's stomach twisted, but he didn't move. This wasn't over.

The figure that entered wasn't who either of them had been expecting. It wasn't Julian. It wasn't even Graham. It was Claire.

Claire walked in like a storm herself, her sharp eyes scanning the room before they landed on Sienna. Her businesslike, calculating demeanor had always made her an outsider in the world of Sienna's café, but tonight, there was something different in her gaze. Her expression was hard, tight, like a woman who had just made a decision that would change everything.

"Sienna," Claire said, her voice all business. "I think it's time we talk."

The Silent Investor

Ethan moved to step away, but Sienna gripped his hand tighter, a silent plea for him to stay. He didn't question it. He didn't want to leave her side now.

"I've been in contact with Perrault," Claire continued, her gaze flickering briefly to Ethan before returning to Sienna. "They've given you an ultimatum. I don't know how much longer we can keep them at bay, Sienna."

Sienna's face hardened at the mention of Perrault, but Claire's words hung in the air like a dark cloud. The tension was so thick, Ethan could practically taste it.

"They're pushing harder now, and if you don't act soon, it'll be too late to salvage anything. The lawyers are coming tomorrow to finalize the buyout. You'll have no choice but to sign. I'm telling you now, Sienna—if you wait, you'll lose this café."

Ethan could see the storm in Sienna's eyes, the raw intensity that had burned there since this all began. She wasn't going to let it happen. She couldn't. But with the pressure mounting, the weight of the decision pressing in on her from all sides, Ethan knew they were at a crossroads.

She turned her gaze to Claire, her voice low but firm. "I don't want to sell. I won't. Not to Perrault. Not to anyone."

Claire's expression didn't change. "It's not up to you anymore, Sienna. It's too late for pride. You're being crushed. It's over."

Sienna's grip tightened on Ethan's hand, her knuckles white.

He could feel her shaking, but she wasn't backing down. Not yet.

"I'm not giving up," she said, her voice barely above a whisper. "Not now. Not when we're this close."

Claire took a step back, her eyes narrowing. "Then you better be ready for the consequences."

The air in the café was thick with impending danger. The moment they were all dreading was upon them.

This was the final hour.

Ethan didn't know what would happen next. But he did know one thing: Whatever it took, he would stand by Sienna. She wasn't alone anymore. Not now. Not when it mattered most.

And they would fight. Together.

Nineteen

Breaking Forth

The café felt like a pressure cooker, the air thick with anticipation and dread. The flickering lights overhead cast long, anxious shadows across the tables, and every ticking second seemed louder than the last. Outside, the world was just beginning to stir. The city, as always, was waking up, people rushing to their jobs, to their lives, to their routines. But inside Sienna's Brew, the world was teetering on the edge of something much darker. The battle for this place had reached its peak.

Sienna stood by the counter, her hands resting on the marble surface, her knuckles pale from the pressure she was exerting on them. Her jaw was set with determination, but her eyes—her eyes held something deeper, something far more dangerous. Fear. She was close to breaking, Ethan could feel it. He had been watching her closely, seeing the cracks in the armor she had built around herself, but now it was like the walls were about to crumble completely.

"Do you want to talk about it?" Ethan asked, his voice low, his words hanging in the air between them. He had tried before to get her to open up, to tell him what was going on inside her head, but each time she had pushed him away. He wasn't about to give up now.

Sienna didn't answer right away. She didn't look at him, didn't acknowledge his presence. The silence stretched out, thick and heavy, as though the world itself was waiting for her to make a decision.

Finally, she spoke, her voice soft but filled with an edge that sent a chill down Ethan's spine. "I don't know how much longer I can do this."

Ethan took a step forward, the words he had been holding back now on the tip of his tongue. "You don't have to do this alone, Sienna."

She turned her head slightly, just enough for him to catch a glimpse of the exhaustion in her eyes. "I've been alone for too long," she said, her voice tight. "I've fought this battle every day for years. But this? I don't know how to keep fighting. Every time I think I've got a chance, something else comes along and drags me back down."

Ethan could see the vulnerability in her—real vulnerability, the kind she had been hiding for so long. He had always known that she was strong, but seeing her like this... he hated it. He wanted to take it all away, to fix it, but he couldn't.

"We'll figure it out," Ethan said, his voice steady, determined. He reached out, his hand gently resting on hers, the warmth of his touch a small comfort in the tense atmosphere. "You're not alone. I'm here."

Sienna didn't pull away, but she didn't respond, either. She simply stared ahead, her mind clearly elsewhere. The decision—the decision to sell or fight, to surrender or stand her ground—was hanging over her like a dark cloud, blocking everything else out.

And then, the door chime rang.

The noise was like a gunshot, sharp and jarring, interrupting the fragile moment between them. Both Sienna and Ethan turned instinctively, their eyes landing on the figure that had stepped inside the café.

It was Graham Hunter.

The man who had been the driving force behind Perrault's takeover efforts. The man who had orchestrated everything, from the pressure on Sienna to the insidious tactics that had been used to force her hand. Ethan could see it in his eyes as he walked in—he was here to finish what he had started.

Sienna stiffened, her posture rigid, her face a mask of resolve. She wasn't going to let him see her flinch. Ethan could feel the change in her, the shift from uncertainty to a kind of cold determination. This was it. This was the final confrontation.

Graham's eyes swept the room, landing on Sienna and Ethan. His smile, though practiced and polite, never quite reached his eyes. The air felt electric with the tension between them. It was like watching a predator approach its prey.

"Ms. Carter," Graham said, his voice smooth, but there was a coldness in it that made the hairs on the back of Ethan's neck stand up. "I've been expecting you to make the right decision. But I can see that you've chosen the hard way, as always."

Sienna didn't flinch, didn't react. She simply stood there, her gaze locked on him, her body tense with a quiet fury that spoke volumes. "I told you, Graham," she said, her voice low but firm, "I'm not selling."

Graham's smile widened, but there was no warmth in it. "That's unfortunate," he said, taking a step toward the counter. "You've had plenty of chances to walk away from this, Sienna. To save yourself. But now you're out of options. The deal is already in motion. You can't stop it."

Sienna's jaw tightened, her hands gripping the counter so hard that her knuckles went white. Ethan could see her struggling to keep it together. She was close to breaking, he could feel it. But she wasn't backing down. Not yet.

"Then do it," she said, her voice low and dangerous. "If you're so sure, go ahead and take it from me. Take it from us."

The words hung in the air, heavy with meaning. Ethan watched Graham closely, his eyes narrowing as he studied the situation. For a moment, it seemed like Graham didn't know how to respond. But then he stepped closer to the counter, his gaze flicking between Sienna and Ethan.

"Very well," Graham said, his voice tinged with a cold amusement. "I see you're not going to make this easy. But mark my words, Sienna. You will lose. And when you do, there will be nothing left but dust and ashes."

Sienna's eyes never left his, and for a moment, there was a silence so thick that it felt like the entire world was holding its breath. Ethan's hand tightened around hers, silently offering her the support she needed. She wasn't alone.

Graham's gaze flicked to Ethan, then back to Sienna. He paused, as if weighing his options, then spoke again, his voice a bit colder. "You're running out of time, Sienna. Perrault doesn't negotiate. You think this little café means something to you, but it doesn't. Perrault has already decided. And you're just a nuisance standing in the way."

"I'm not moving," Sienna said, her voice cutting through the silence like a blade. "I'm standing my ground. And I'll fight this to the end."

Graham's eyes narrowed, his lips twisting into a sneer. "We'll see about that."

With one final glance, Graham turned and walked toward the

Breaking Forth

door, his footsteps echoing with the certainty that this was far from over. The door swung shut behind him with a sharp, almost final sound, leaving Sienna and Ethan alone once again in the stillness of the café.

For a long moment, neither of them spoke. Ethan could feel the weight of everything pressing down on them—on Sienna, on him, on everything they had been fighting for. Sienna was standing at the edge of something much darker than she had ever imagined. But she wasn't backing down.

"I won't let them win," Sienna whispered, her voice tight with emotion. "I won't let him take this from me."

Ethan stepped forward, his hand resting gently on her arm. "You don't have to fight alone, Sienna. You're not alone in this."

Her eyes met his then, searching his face, as if looking for something she wasn't sure she would find. But there was no doubt in his eyes. No hesitation. He was with her.

"I don't know how much longer I can do this," she said quietly, the vulnerability in her voice that she had tried so hard to hide breaking through. "But I know I can't let go of this place. I can't let them take it from me."

Ethan nodded. "We fight together. Whatever happens next, we do it together."

The weight of her decision hung heavy between them, but for the first time in a long time, Sienna didn't look so lost. She didn't look so alone. She looked like she was ready to face whatever was coming next.

The storm wasn't over. Not by a long shot. But they would stand together.

And they would fight to the very end.

Twenty

Final Decision

The café felt smaller than usual, as if the walls were closing in around them, suffocating them under the weight of the final hours. The clock on the wall ticked loudly in the stillness of the room, each second marking the dwindling time they had before Perrault's lawyers arrived to finalize the deal. Sienna could feel the ticking, the pressure mounting with every passing minute, but she refused to back down.

Ethan stood beside her, his eyes constantly on her, but he knew better than to push her. He knew she was at a breaking point—he could see it in her posture, in the way her eyes darted around the room, as if searching for an answer that didn't exist. The night had been long, filled with sleepless moments and broken conversations, and now it was almost over. The choice had already been made; the deal was there, the papers were ready to sign. Everything she had fought for was now within reach, but at what cost?

Her hands were shaking as she gripped the counter, her fingers wrapped tightly around the edge. She wasn't aware of it, but Ethan could see it, the subtle tremor in her fingertips, the way she clenched her fists at her sides like she was holding something back. There was a coldness in the air that didn't belong, a shift in the mood, and it was all because of what was coming. What would happen next.

"We don't have much time," Ethan said softly, breaking the silence that had stretched for what felt like hours. He didn't know what more to say—everything had been said. But the reality of the situation was beginning to sink in, and he wasn't sure they could keep fighting like this forever. "Are you ready?"

Sienna's head snapped up, and for the first time in what felt like forever, her eyes met his. There was a storm in them, a swirl of emotions so intense that it nearly knocked the breath out of him. She wasn't just fighting for the café anymore. She wasn't just holding onto a place; she was holding onto her life, her identity, everything she had left.

"I'm ready," she said quietly, but the words were laced with doubt, uncertainty. "I don't know if I'm ready, but I can't let them win."

Her voice was steady, but the cracks were there, hidden behind the resolve. Ethan could hear the fear, the fear that had been haunting her for so long, and he hated it. He hated seeing her like this, torn between fighting for something that had been her entire world and realizing that there was no guarantee she would win. But if she gave up now, she would lose everything—not just the café, but herself.

She turned away from him, her eyes scanning the papers on the counter. The contract that had been sitting there for days now seemed to mock her, its clean lines and professional language a reminder of how out of control she was. It was just a piece of paper, but it held her future in its ink.

Ethan moved closer to her, not saying anything for a moment, just standing beside her. He could feel the heat of her body, the way her muscles were tense with the weight of what was to come. He could feel her fear, but more than that, he could feel her determination, and it terrified him. Because he didn't know how far she was willing to go. He didn't know if she could walk away without losing everything that mattered to her.

"You don't have to do this," he said softly, his voice barely above a whisper. He didn't know why he was saying it. Maybe it was the desperation in her eyes, or the way her shoulders were trembling under the strain of the moment. "You don't have to make this decision."

Sienna's eyes flickered to him, her gaze cold, her expression unreadable. She pulled her hand back from the counter, her fingers brushing over the contract once more. She didn't respond immediately, and for a moment, Ethan thought she might walk away, retreat into herself again. But she didn't.

"I have to make it," she said, her voice tight with emotion. "I have no choice. They've already won, Ethan. They're going to take this place from me, and I can't stop it. I can't fight this anymore. It's too late."

The finality in her voice sent a chill through him. She was giving up. He couldn't let her. Not like this. Not after everything they had been through together.

"You're not giving up," Ethan said firmly, stepping in front of her. He placed his hands on her shoulders, forcing her to meet his eyes. "You're not done yet. We still have a chance to fight. We're not out of options."

Sienna looked at him, her eyes searching his face for something, for anything that would make her believe it. "And what do you want me to do, Ethan?" she asked, her voice thick with emotion. "What do you want me to do when everything is falling apart? When the people who are supposed to help me are the ones trying to destroy me?"

Ethan took a deep breath, feeling the weight of her words settle over him like a fog. He didn't have all the answers. He didn't know how they were going to win this battle. But he knew one thing: she wasn't alone. Not anymore. He wasn't going to let her carry this burden by herself.

"I want you to know that no matter what happens, I'm here with you," he said quietly. "I'll stand by you, Sienna. And I'll help you fight this. I won't let you go down without a fight."

Sienna's breath hitched, the fear in her eyes momentarily flickering as she seemed to absorb his words. For a brief second, there was a flash of something vulnerable in her—the person she had hidden so carefully, the person who was scared and unsure and lost.

"I don't know how to do this anymore," she whispered, her voice trembling. "I don't know how to fight them. I don't know if I can win."

Ethan stepped closer, gently brushing a stray lock of hair from her face. He could see the storm in her eyes, the doubt that had crept into her, the fear that maybe, just maybe, this time, she was going to lose.

"You don't have to do this alone," he repeated softly, his hand resting on hers, gently urging her to look up at him. "Whatever happens next, we do it together."

For a long moment, Sienna didn't respond. She simply stood there, her eyes searching his face, as if trying to find something to hold onto. Slowly, the tension seemed to drain from her shoulders, the fear slowly melting away as she took in the warmth of his words. But still, there was doubt, that nagging sense of what if?

And then, the door opened again.

The chime rang sharply in the silence, and both of them turned toward it. Sienna's body stiffened, and Ethan felt his own heart skip a beat.

The Silent Investor

It was Claire.

Her eyes flicked to them both, sharp and calculating. She walked in with the same businesslike confidence she had always carried, but this time, there was something else in her demeanor—something darker, more urgent. She wasn't here to offer comfort. She was here to deliver the news. And Ethan could feel the air in the room grow even heavier as she approached.

"I've spoken with the lawyers," Claire said, her voice firm but tinged with something that could only be called concern. "Perrault is pushing hard. They want to finalize the deal tomorrow morning. If you don't act now, it's over. The café is done."

Sienna's face paled, but there was no panic in her expression. There was nothing but quiet resolve.

"I've made my decision," Sienna said, her voice steady. "I'm not selling. I'm not giving up."

Claire didn't say anything for a moment, just looked at her, her eyes searching Sienna's face. Finally, she spoke, her voice softer now. "You're not going to win this fight, Sienna. They're too big. They'll bury you. You'll lose everything—this café, everything you've built. And I can't be the one to watch it happen. I can't be the one to let you destroy yourself."

Sienna turned to face her, her gaze hardening. "I'm not destroying myself. I'm fighting for what's mine. What I've built. And I'm not letting anyone take it from me."

Ethan could feel the weight of the moment pressing down on both of them. This was the final decision. There was no going back.

But Sienna wasn't backing down. Not now.

She reached for the contract on the counter, her fingers brushing against it once more, but this time, she didn't hesitate.

She ripped it in half.

The sound of the paper tearing was loud, final. The last of Perrault's offer lay in shreds on the counter, the pieces scattered across the marble like the remnants of a battle already fought.

"We fight this together," Sienna said, her voice unwavering. "And I don't care what happens. We're not giving up. Not now."

Ethan looked at her, his chest swelling with pride. This was it. They were past the breaking point. They had made their decision.

And now, there was no turning back.

www.ingramcontent.com/pod-product-compliance
Lightning Source LLC
LaVergne TN
LVHW011946070526
838202LV00054B/4826